W9-BXW-690
3 3090 00373 8980

CULTURES OF THE WORLD
Laos

Fremont Public Library
1170 N. Midlothian Road
Mundelein, IL 60060

Cavendish
Square
New York

Published in 2018 by Cavendish Square Publishing, LLC
243 5th Avenue, Suite 136, New York, NY 10016

Copyright © 2018 by Cavendish Square Publishing, LLC
Third Edition

No part of this publication may be reproduced, stored in a retrieval system, or transmitted in any form or by any means—electronic, mechanical, photocopying, recording, or otherwise—without the prior permission of the copyright owner. Request for permission should be addressed to Permissions, Cavendish Square Publishing, 243 5th Avenue, Suite 136, New York, NY 10016. Tel (877) 980-4450; fax (877) 980-4454.
Website: cavendishsq.com

This publication represents the opinions and views of the author based on his or her personal experience, knowledge, and research. The information in this book serves as a general guide only. The author and publisher have used their best efforts in preparing this book and disclaim liability rising directly or indirectly from the use and application of this book.

All websites were available and accurate when this book was sent to press.

Library of Congress Cataloging-in-Publication Data

Names: Mansfield, Stephen, author. | Koh, Magdalene, author. | Nevins,
Debbie, author.
Title: Laos / Stephen Mansfield, Magdalene Koh, Debbie Nevins.
Description: New York : Cavendish Square Publishing, 2018. | Series: Cultures of the world (third edition) | Includes bibliographical references
and index. | Audience: Grades 5-8.
Identifiers: LCCN 2017047200 (print) | LCCN 2017047980 (ebook) | ISBN 9781502632333 (library bound) | ISBN 9781502632340 (ebook)
Subjects: LCSH: Laos--Juvenile works.
Classification: LCC DS555.3 (ebook) | LCC DS555.3 .M37 2018 (print) | DDC
959.4--dc23
LC record available at https://lccn.loc.gov/2017047200

Writers, Stephen Mansfield, Magdalene Koh; Debbie Nevins, third edition
Editorial Director, third edition: David McNamara
Editor, third edition: Debbie Nevins
Art Director, third edition: Amy Greenan
Designer, third edition: Jessica Nevins
Picture Researcher, third edition: Jessica Nevins

PICTURE CREDITS
The photographs in this book are used with the permission of: **Cover Godong/UIG via Getty Images**; p.1 Muellek Josef/Shutterstock.com; p. 3 nuwatphoto/Shutterstock.com; p. 5 faizol musa/Shutterstock.com; p. 6 Avigator Thailand/Shutterstock.com; p. 7 Megapress/Alamy Stock Photo; p. 8 dikobraziy/Shutterstock.com; p. 10 Worakit Sirijinda/Shutterstock.com; p. 11 lakatos/Shutterstock.com; p. 12 Ozerov Alexander/Shutterstock.com; p. 13 sarintra chimphoolsuk/Shutterstock.com; p. 14 Matyas Rehak/Shutterstock.com; p. 15 meunierd/Shutterstock.com; p. 16 apiguide/Shutterstock.com; p. 17 Suriya99/Shutterstock.com; p. 18 meunierd/Shutterstock.com; p. 20 Andrew McConnell/Alamy Stock Photo; p. 22 Stanislav Fosenbauer/Shutterstock.com; p. 23 Chaoborus/Wikimedia Commons/File:Fa Ngum-Vtne1.JPG/CC BY-SA 3.0; p. 25 Keystone/Hulton Archive/Getty Images; p. 26 Bettmann/Getty Images; p. 27 Bettmann/Getty Images; p. 28 frerd/Shutterstock.com; p. 30 © Liu Ailun/Xinhua/Alamy Live News; p. 33 loca4motion/Shutterstock.com; p. 34 User:DTR/Wikimedia Commons/File:Emblem of Laos.svg; p. 36 Siri Te/Shutterstock.com; p. 38 Athapet Piruksa/Shutterstock.com; p. 39 BePhumirat/Shutterstock.com; p. 40 kwanchai/Shutterstock.com; p. 41 C. Na Songkhla/Shutterstock.com; p. 42 Saylakham/Shutterstock.com; p. 43 Nawin nachiangmai/Shutterstock.com; p. 44 Don Mammoser/Shutterstock.com; p. 45 lovely pet/Shutterstock.com; p. 46 Don Mammoser/Shutterstock.com; p. 47 Alexander Mazurkevich/Shutterstock.com; p. 48 OneShotImage/Shutterstock.com; p. 50 luck luckyfarm/Shutterstock.com; p. 52 Jerry Redfern/LightRocket via Getty Images; p. 53 Wasuta23/Shutterstock.com; p. 54 Kizuna Chanthavong/Shutterstock.com; p. 55 Jerry Redfern/LightRocket via Getty Images; p. 56 Wolfgang Kaehler/LightRocket via Getty Images; p. 58 Sirisak_baokaew/Shutterstock.com; p. 60 Ben Davies/LightRocket via Getty Images; p. 61 Muellek Josef/Shutterstock.com; p. 62 marclafond/Alamy Stock Photo; p. 63 Avigator Thailand/Shutterstock.com; p. 64 In Pictures Ltd./Corbis via Getty Images; p. 66 Phoutthavong SOUVANNACHAK/Shutterstock.com; p. 69 SantiPhotoSS/Shutterstock.com; p. 70 rweisswald/Shutterstock.com; p. 71 Oxana Mamlina/Shutterstock.com; p. 72 sarintra chimphoolsuk/Shutterstock.com; p. 73 Rafal Cichawa/Shutterstock.com; p. 74 rweisswald/Shutterstock.com; p. 75 In Pictures Ltd./Corbis via Getty Images; p. 76 age fotostock/Alamy Stock Photo; p. 78 Gougnaf/Shutterstock.com; p. 80 phetsamay philavanh/Shutterstock.com; p. 82 Champiofoto/Shutterstock.com; p. 85 rweisswald/Shutterstock.com; p. 86 baldovina/Shutterstock.com; p. 88 Worldpics/Shutterstock.com; p. 90 GuitarM/Shutterstock.com; p. 91 Andrii Lutsyk/Shutterstock.com; p. 92 Sidhe/Shutterstock.com; p. 93 Tunyou/Shutterstock.com; p. 94 Gail Palethorpe/Shutterstock.com; p. 96 Moolkum/Shutterstock.com; p. 98 Robert Nickelsberg/The LIFE Images Collection/Getty Images; p. 99 Peter4940/Wikimedia Commons/File:Monk holding bundles of Sinxay palm leaf manuscripts while pointing to a painting of Sinxay within the sim.jpg/CC BY-SA 4.0; p. 100 Maiphone yang/Shutterstock.com; p. 101 magicinfoto/Shutterstock.com; p. 102 Anirut Thailand/Shutterstock.com; p. 103 owen1978/Shutterstock.com; p. 104 amadeustx/Shutterstock.com; p. 105 wolffpower/Shutterstock.com; p. 106 Tepikina Nastya/Shutterstock.com; p. 108 Stefano Ember/Shutterstock.com; p. 110 Leisa Tyler/LightRocket via Getty Images; p. 111 HOANG DINH NAM/AFP/Getty Images; p. 112 Chau Doan/LightRocket via Getty Images; p. 113 Dietmar Temps/Shutterstock.com; p. 114 HOANG DINH NAM/AFP/Getty Images; p. 116 hikarurin/Shutterstock.com; p. 118 Peter Stuckings/Shutterstock.com; p. 119 bonga1965/Shutterstock.com; p. 121 LILLIAN SUWANRUMPHA/AFP/Getty Images; p. 122 Tee11/Shutterstock.com; p. 124 enmyo/Shutterstock.com; p. 125 Matyas Rehak/Shutterstock.com; p. 126 Andrii Lutsyk/Shutterstock.com; p. 127 Ben Davies/LightRocket via Getty Images; p. 128 Ricard MC/Shutterstock.com; p. 129 MemoryMan/Shutterstock.com; p. 130 C_KAWI/Shutterstock.com; p. 131 f8grapher/Shutterstock.com.

PRECEDING PAGE:
The Patuxai war memorial in Ventiane commemorates the lives of those who died fighting France.

Printed in the United States of America

CONTENTS

LAOS TODAY

LAOS IS SOMETIMES CALLED "THE FORGOTTEN COUNTRY." Perhaps it's because it is a fairly quiet country that many outsiders can't quite locate or visualize in their minds. Or maybe it's because in this mostly rural country, where farmers still use water buffalo to pull plows, it can seem like time itself has forgotten this place. Yet again, it could be that while the world was riveted by the calamitous Vietnam War during the 1960s and 1970s, it was on "forgotten" Laos that most bombs fell, a humanitarian disaster toward which many Westerners turned a blind eye.

Even today, many Americans don't know what happened in Laos in those years, or that the Lao people are still being killed by those bombs, to the tune of about one hundred fatalities each year. Many people don't know that Laos has the dubious distinction of being the single-most bombed country per-capita in global history.

Given the country's long history, however, perhaps that shouldn't be so surprising. The fate of Laos resembles that of a pawn. First embattled, then conquered, and eventually abandoned, Laos has a history filled with much bloodshed and hardship. Ancient civilizations competed to subdue its kingdoms. Colonial masters raced to

Hmong women dress in traditional costumes for the festival season in Xiangkhouang.

gain possession and bragging rights. Superpowers sparred to advance their ideologies for ultimate dominion. Caught in the crossfire, the country is still one of the least developed in the world.

Despite such adversity, Laos's rich heritage and wealth of natural resources have remained largely intact. Remote villages maintain their self-sufficient ways, ethnic groups still weave colorful costumes, and entire communities carry on celebrating both animist and Buddhist festivities. Life marches on according to the ebb and flow of the seasons, as the nation rebuilds itself socially, economically, and psychologically.

Nevertheless, there are obstacles to Laos's full expression of itself as a nation. Despite the government's recent embrace of Buddhist tradition and support for more private sector goods and services, Laos remains a Communist country. This is particularly notable in the government's strict control of the media. In fact, the government owns all newspapers and broadcast media. Although the nation's constitution guarantees freedom of the press, public criticism of government or party leaders is a criminal offense, as is the reporting of any news that "weakens the state," or the importing of a publication that is "contrary to national culture."

In 2014, the Laotian government passed a new law extending those restrictions to the internet. So far, however, the authorities's technical abilities to monitor internet use are limited, so enforcement of the law may not be up to the job. But that doesn't mean it won't catch up. At this time, there isn't much noticeable dissent anyway, which either means everyone in Laos is content, or that self-censorship is pervasive. On the other hand, internet use is low to begin with, although younger people, particularly in urban areas, are increasingly using social media. It may only be a matter of time before the discussion of sensitive political and social issues picks up. Nevertheless, the government is eager to boost Laos's information and communication technology capabilities, and in 2014, the country's first state-funded nationwide underground fiber optic network was completed.

A sign advertises the *Vientiane Mai* newspaper.

While that is commendable news, to be sure, it's worth noting that Laos is an extremely poor country, where many people still don't have electricity, never mind fast internet service. Although it has enjoyed economic growth in recent years, it's still the poorest country in Southeast Asia, and barely beats the impoverished nations of sub-Saharan Africa on many economic lists.

The government, one of the world's few remaining communist regimes, is working hard to attract foreign investment, particularly in boosting the country's hydropower capabilities. This, it hopes, along with increased tourism, will pull Laos up out of poverty and transform it into a major economic power in Southeast Asia, unlikely to be forgotten again.

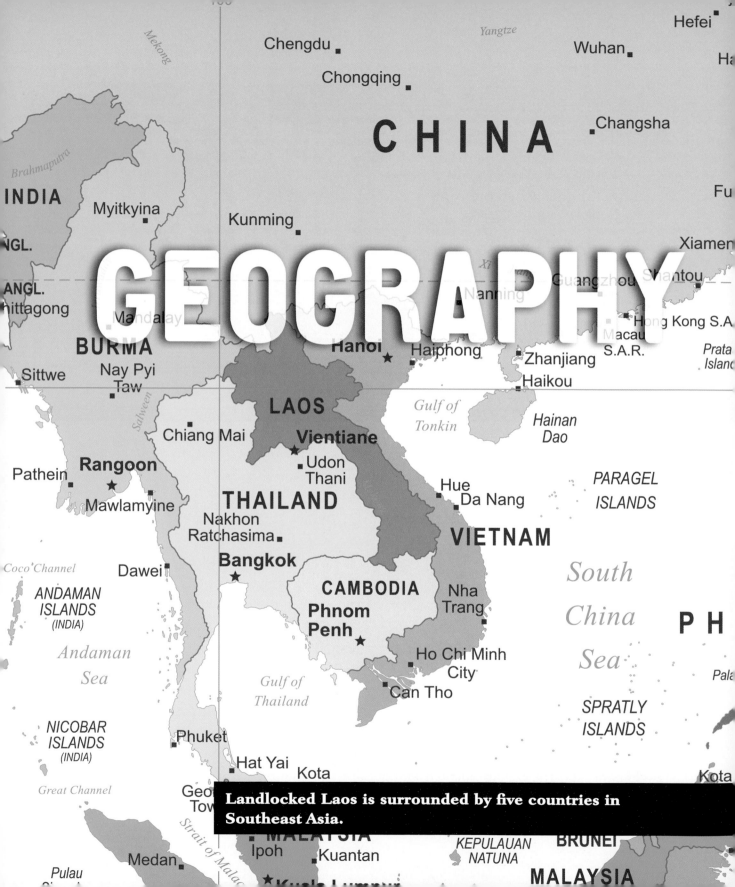

GEOGRAPHY

Landlocked Laos is surrounded by five countries in Southeast Asia.

1

LAOS IS A COUNTRY OF MIST-shrouded mountains, lush tropical rainforests, emerald rice fields, and blue lagoons. Towering bronze Buddhas and saffron-robed monks. It is golden temples and rickety wooden houseboats on the mighty Mekong River. Laos is curries with sticky rice and French baguettes. It is a tranquil, unhurried place—and is also, per capita, the most heavily bombed nation on earth.

Laos is the only landlocked country in Southeast Asia, a subcontinent made up of more water than land. It's the least populated country in the region and, with a landmass of only 91,429 square miles (236,800 square kilometers)—about twice the size Pennsylvania, but shaped like a windblown tree—it is also one of the smallest. Laos's diverse frontiers, however, give the impression of a country that extends far and wide.

The country is bordered on the north by the Chinese province of Yunnan, on the northeast by Vietnam, on the northwest by Myanmar (Burma), on the west by Thailand, and to the south by Cambodia. Laos's landscape is dominated by the mountains of the north and east, as well as the great Mekong River and its tributaries. The high plateau of Xiangkhoang and the rolling Bolaven Plateau are the country's other main geographical features.

Laos is roughly 600 miles (966 km) long and 330 miles (531 km) across at its widest point, in the far northwest. In the narrowest part of the southern panhandle it is only 100 miles (161 km) wide, tightly walled in by the land bulges of Thailand and Cambodia. Military and colonial history has determined these borders, and in the process, denied Laos access to the sea.

The dramatic scenery of Vang Vieng attracts tourists to this river town.

THE FLOODPLAINS

About 70 percent of Laos is covered with rugged mountains and forested hills. Only the river plains and the shallow valleys can be cultivated for food production. However, such arable land is limited and consists of just 4 percent of Laos's total terrain.

During the rainy season, the Mekong River carries great quantities of fertile silt, contributing to the region's agricultural wealth. The annual flooding of the river and its tributaries during the monsoon season ensures enough sustained moisture for wet-rice cultivation. The combination of tropical heat and rich topsoil deposits by the river has turned these floodplains into intensely fertile areas. Glutinous rice, which is the staple food of the Lao, is cultivated on these areas. Provided there are no disastrous crop failures, the floodplains can serve the entire country's rice requirements.

The rivers are also an important source of fish. The generosity of these plains and the proximity of the life-giving Mekong explain why the majority of Lao live on or near the plains. Most of Laos's key cities are also located there.

The Lao have come to rely on the age-old seasonal patterns of flooding that have enriched their farms. In recent years, however, the over-logging of forests located on mountain slopes, particularly in the north, has caused water levels to change. This threatens the livelihoods of the lowland Lao farmers. Further exacerbating the water situation is the construction of dams on the tributaries of the Mekong River and in the Yunnan Province.

THE PLATEAUS

The only other level land of any sort, apart from the floodplains, is on the mountain plateaus. The largest, the Xiangkhoang Plateau, is in the northern province of Xiangkhoang.

This vast area of rolling hills and grassland reaches an average altitude of about 4,250 feet (1,295 meters). Phou Bia, which at 9,252 feet (2,820 m) is Laos's highest peak, rises at the plateau's southern edge. The soil here is poor, yielding few crops.

The central part of the plateau, an area of extensive grassland that supports an occasional tree, is better known as the Plain of Jars, or Thong Hai Hin. The name comes from the hundreds of stone vessels that remain scattered over the plain. The jars are roughly two thousand years old, weigh between 4,000 and 6,000 pounds (1,814 and 2,722 kilograms), and measure between 1 and 8 feet (0.3 and 2.4 m) in height and 3 feet (0.9 m) in diameter.

Long vistas can be seen across the Xiangkhoang Plateau.

The Tad E-Tu waterfall is one of many in Laos.

The Khammouan Plateau is a beautiful area of limestone hills, rivers, jungle-smothered gorges, and underground grottoes located between the Annamese Cordillera and the Mekong. The larger Bolaven Plateau lies in the southeast corner of the country's southern panhandle. A cooler altitude, plentiful rain, and fertile earth make the Bolaven Plateau, along with the lowland plains, one of the most productive agricultural areas in Laos. In addition to rice, fruits such as pineapples, durians, and peaches, all kinds of vegetables, and tobacco are cultivated on the plateau. During the French colonial period the area was well known for its rubber and coffee production. Decades of war and neglect have left much of this region in ruins, but in recent years coffee has become an important export for the country. The rubber plantations, however, continue to languish.

THE MIGHTY MEKONG

The Mekong is one of the twelve great rivers of the world and the longest waterway in Southeast Asia. It flows for 2,800 miles (4,506 km) through six countries. From its source in the highlands of Tibet, it passes through China, Myanmar, Laos, Thailand, and Cambodia before flowing into Vietnam's Mekong Delta and out to the South China Sea.

Of all the Mekong countries, Laos occupies the longest stretch of the river. The Mekong and its tributaries run throughout the country and provide a much-needed source of fish, and its narrow floodplains enrich Laos's agriculture. Its waters carry tankers and barges, ferries, houseboats, pirogues, and sampans that provide transportation to people and freight along the length of the country.

Only a little more than half of the Lao section of the Mekong is navigable all year. Some of the northern stretches of the river—where there are rapids in the wet months and sharp, exposed rocks during the dry—can be navigated only for about six months of the year, and even then only by flat-bottomed boats.

The Mekong enters Laos through a narrow, 125-mile (201-km) gorge that slices through rugged mountains along the country's border with Burma. The river widens a little farther east as it is joined by one of its largest tributaries. It then courses past the cities of Luang Prabang (also spelled Louangphrabang) and Vientiane, and then onward to the southern cities of Savannakhet and Pakse. The river is navigable only as far as the Khone Falls, near the Cambodian border, where a massive natural barrier of rocks and rapids forms a series of thundering cascades.

WORLD HERITAGE SITES

Since 1975, the United Nations Educational, Scientific and Cultural Organization (UNESCO) has maintained a list of international landmarks or regions considered to be of "outstanding value" to the people of the world. Such sites embody the common natural and cultural heritage of humanity, and therefore deserve particular protection. The organization works with the host country to establish plans for managing and conserving their sites. UNESCO also reports on sites which are in imminent or potential danger of destruction and can offer emergency funds to try to save the property.

The Wat Phu Champasak temple in Laos.

The organization is continually assessing new sites to inclusion on the World Heritage list. In order to be selected, a site much be of "outstanding universal value" and meet at least one of ten criteria. These required elements include cultural value—that is, artistic, religious, or historical significance—and natural value, including exceptional beauty, unusual natural phenomenon, and scientific importance.

As of July 2017, 1073 sites have been listed, including 832 cultural, 206 natural, and 35 mixed properties in 167 nations. Two are in Laos—the Town of Luang Prabang, and Vat Phou and Associated Ancient Settlements within the Champasak Landscape.

THE ANNAMESE CORDILLERA

A spur of the Himalayas that runs from Tibet to Vietnam, the Annamese Cordillera, or Annam Highlands, is Indochina's main north-south divide. The chain runs almost the entire length of Laos. The rugged northern mountains and hills form a series of steep, sharp parallel folds and ridges where rivers run through deep gorges. These mountains rise from 5,000 to almost 10,000 feet (1,524—3,048 m). The chain begins in the northwest of Laos and levels out in the southeast, dividing the watersheds of the region's eastern- and southern-flowing rivers.

CLIMATE

The temperatures are generally tropical to subtropical in Laos, depending on the altitude, the latitude, and the monsoon. The rainy season runs from May to October. The temperatures at this time are as high as 80° Fahrenheit (27° Celsius) and above.

The Mekong River becomes a dry riverbed in parts of Vientiane during the hot, dry season.

In mountainous regions such as Xiangkhouang, temperatures can drop to freezing in December and January. The hottest months are March and April, when temperatures soar into the high 90s on the Fahrenheit scale (high 30s° C). The coolest months are November to February, the first part of the dry season. The level of the Mekong drops dramatically at this time, revealing little islands and sandbanks that are submerged for the rest of the year. These are eagerly appropriated by the Lao and turned into attractive kitchen gardens for the cultivation of cucumbers, tomatoes, beans, pumpkins, and other vegetables and fruits.

Rainfall varies considerably throughout Laos. The mountainous northern province of Luang Prabang receives an average of about 50 inches (127 centimeters) of rain annually, while the Bolaven Plateau in the south averages 100 inches (254 cm). The wet months vary. In Vientiane, they are from May to September, whereas in Luang Prabang, August is far wetter than any other month.

Many cultural events are connected with the seasons and the climate. For example, the Rocket Festival, or Boun Bang Fay, in May sees the launching of giant homemade rockets that were believed to reach the heavens and bring back a deluge of rain. In addition, the end of the harvest season is a popular time for weddings and village festivals.

At the confluence of the Mekong and the Nam Khan Rivers in northern Laos lies the colorful town of Luang Prabang. The ancient royal capital is the country's premier tourist destination and one of its two UNESCO World Heritage Sites.

Luang Prabang was selected as a World Heritage Site because, according to UNESCO, "it is an outstanding example of the fusion of traditional architecture and Lao urban structures with those built by the European colonial authorities in the nineteenth and twentieth centuries. Its unique, remarkably well-preserved townscape illustrates a key stage in the blending of these two distinct cultural traditions."

The historical section of the town contains thirty-three richly decorated wats, or Buddhist temples—most famously the Wat Xieng Thong ("Temple of the Golden City"), which dates to 1560. The town remains an authentic center of religious and spiritual study, where saffron-robed monks are a common sight. Surrounding the town are mountains, waterfalls, elephant sanctuaries, rice paddies, and jungles.

FLORA AND FAUNA

Laos's forests are among its greatest assets. A varied species of tropical and subtropical trees cover almost half of the country. Deciduous trees and hardwood forests are found on the slopes of mountains and rain forest vegetation in jungle areas. In the north there are mixed forests with large stands of evergreens, oaks, and pines. In the cultivated lowlands of the south, mango and palm trees are common. On large plateaus such as the Plain of Jars, grassy savannas prevail.

Much of this green heritage is being threatened by illegal logging and commercial plantations. Many indigenous groups from the hills practice shifting cultivation, also known as swidden agriculture or slash-and-burn agriculture. Before any planting can begin, this harmful method of farming requires large tracks of land to be set on fire and then cleared with axes and hoes. The ashes add valuable nutrients for the crops. When the soil's nutrients are exhausted, the farmers move on to another piece of land, leaving the abandoned fields fallow for about fifteen years.

Many animals, including some rare species, live in the mountains and jungles of Laos. These include tigers, leopards, rhinoceroses, lemurs, gibbons, several kinds of deer (including barking deer), wild pigs, crocodiles, cobras, kraits, and a wide variety of birdlife such as eagles, bulbuls, hornbills, pheasants, and hawks. Water buffaloes and elephants are trained to work. Elephants are used to haul large tree trunks from the forests down to rivers and roads. Traditionally elephants were used in the transportation of soldiers

A tired child rests on a water buffalo while his father tills the rice field.

and supplies in wartime. The Khone Falls of the Mekong in southern Laos is home to the rare and endangered species of freshwater dolphins. In the more remote areas of Laos, chickens, pigs, and even buffaloes are still offered in sacrifices to the gods, spirits, and ancestors of the village.

Every year several tons of endangered species are smuggled out of the country. This illegal trade of wildlife is ever growing and increasingly profitable.

THE CITIES

By Southeast Asian standards, Vientiane, with a population of about 760,000 (in 2015), is a small capital. In 1563, King Setthathirat (also spelled Setthathirath) founded the capital, then known as Vieng Chan, to protect his kingdom against invasion. A former Buddhist center, the capital was raided and burned to the ground by the Siamese (Thai) in 1827 and was at

The great golden stupa of the Pha That Luang pagoda is the most important national monument in Laos.

the mercy of the jungle for several decades before the French took control of the country.

The Friendship Bridge, completed in 1994, connects the Thai town of Nong Khai with Tha Nalaeng, a Lao river port, providing a further spur to economic change and development.

The three main urban centers apart from Vientiane are Savannakhet, Luang Prabang, and Pakse. Luang Prabang is the former royal capital and was named a World Heritage city by UNESCO in 1995. Savannakhet is near the Thai border and is an important trading post.

INTERNET LINKS

http://www.bbc.com/travel/story/20150810-laos-strange-plain-of-jars
This article provides photos and a bit of history about the mysterious Plain of Jars.

https://www.lonelyplanet.com/laos
This travel site has many impressive photos of Laos and its various geographical areas and attractions.

http://whc.unesco.org/en/list/479
This World Heritage listing for Luang Prabang has a media link at the bottom for a video.

http://whc.unesco.org/en/list/481
The World Heritage listing page for Vat Phou includes slides and a video.

HISTORY

An unexploded cluster bomb left over from the Vietnam War is detonated in Sam Neua under controlled conditions by the Lao National Unexploded Ordnance Programme (UXO Lao).

2

P EOPLE LIVED IN THE REGION OF THE Lower Mekong Basin as long as ten thousand years ago, but there are no written accounts of the early history of Laos. Legends come before historical facts. For the ethnic minorities of Laos in particular, most of whom have no written records of their own, legends remain the only real way of explaining and passing down information about their origins.

Legends about the origins of the Lao people take many forms. The best-known account narrates how the King of Heaven sent the first ancestor of the Lao, Khun Borom, to rule over the land. Seated on a white elephant, Khun Borom discovered a vine bearing two giant gourds. When these were pierced, men, women, animals, and seeds poured out. Using these resources to establish their own domains, Khun Borom's seven sons divided the land among themselves, thus founding seven Tai principalities.

EARLY MIGRATIONS

At this point historical facts and legends begin to merge. The Lao are a branch of the Tai people, who occupied a large area of Yunnan Province in China, long before recorded history.

The geographical position of Laos has always been central to its history. Surrounded by stronger and more ambitious nations, the country has been constrained by the Annamese Cordillera to the east and the Mekong River to the west. Its history can be described as a continuous struggle to keep its political unity and to maintain a strong national identity of its own.

One of Laos' oldest—and strangest—connections to its ancient past is the mysterious Plain of Jars, or Thong Hai Hin. Located on the Xiangkhoang Plateau in the north central part of the country, it is a megalithic archaeological landscape dating from about 500 BCE to 500 CE. Scattered over about ninety sites in the hilly terrain are more than two thousand large stone vessels, or jars, and fragments of others. The tallest jars are nearly 10 feet (3 meters) high, and most of the vessels are carved of sandstone, granite, or calcified coral.

Though little is known about the civilization that created these urns, or their purpose, archaeologists believe the jars probably served as burial or cremation vessels. The fields they rest in would have been ancient cemeteries. Burned human bone fragments and teeth, along with colored glass beads were found inside some of the jars, while unburned human remains, pottery fragments, iron and bronze objects, and more glass and stone beads were found surrounding them.

The Field of Jars region was heavily bombed during the "Secret War" years, and many sites remain riddled with unexploded ordnance (UXO). Most are too dangerous to open to tourists. Jar Sites 1, 2, and 3, the most popular sites, were searched and cleared in 2004–2005 by the British-based Mines Advisory Group (MAG), and several other jar sites have been cleared more recently. But large signs caution against walking through the remaining areas. In light of the heavy bombardment this extraordinary archaeological region endured in the 1960s and 1970s, it's astonishing that as many of these ancient treasures survived as did. The Lao PDR government has applied for the Plain of Jars to be granted status as a UNESCO World Heritage Site.

The name *Lao* appears first in Chinese and Vietnamese annals during the shadowy period between the third and fourteenth centuries when the Tai peoples were migrating from Central Asia into southern China. By the eighth century, they had established the strong military kingdom of Nan Chao in Yunnan.

These Tai tribes continued moving toward the borders of present-day Laos, Vietnam, Thailand, and Burma. The pace of this slow, southward migration from Yunnan gathered momentum in the thirteenth century with the fall of Ta-li, the capital of Nan Chao, to the armies of Kublai Khan.

LAND OF A MILLION ELEPHANTS

The recorded history of Laos begins one hundred years after the fall of Nan Chao with the birth of Fa Ngum in 1316. Fa Ngum, a Lao prince, grew up in exile at the court of Angkor in Cambodia. It was here that he studied and later adopted the Buddhist faith and married a Khmer princess.

With the help of the Cambodian king, Fa Ngum succeeded in uniting the Lao kingdom of Champasak in the south, Xieng Khuang in the northeast, the kingdom of Muang Swa and its royal city, Luang Prabang, in the north, and the kingdom of Viang Chan, as Vientiane was then called. This brilliant warrior was also a champion of Buddhism, a creed that he established as the state religion.

Under his rule, the borders of the country were extended to include large parts of southwest Yunnan, eastern Siam (Thailand), the Korat Plateau, and most of present-day Laos. Fa Ngum named the kingdom Lan Xang, the "Land of a Million Elephants."

The work of Fa Ngum was continued by Samsenthai (1373—1416), his son, and the other rulers who followed. In 1563 King Setthathirat moved the capital from Luang Prabang to Vieng Chan. A number of palaces, libraries, Buddhist temples, and monuments were built at this time.

A statue of Fa Ngum is a popular landmark in Vientiane.

After Setthathirat's death in 1571, Burma invaded the kingdom, which then fell into anarchy. After the arrival of King Souligna Vongsa (1637—94), a long period of peace and security followed, heralding Lan Xang's golden age. Ruling for 57 years, the longest reign of any Lao monarch, Souligna Vongsa further expanded his kingdom's territory and power.

At the height of its power, Lan Xang also achieved fame as a center of Buddhist learning, attracting monks and scholars from Siam, Burma, and Cambodia. It was at this time that the first Europeans visited the country.

THE DECLINE OF LAN XANG

The decline of Lan Xang began with Souligna Vongsa's death. In the absence of a male heir to the throne, the country soon split into three separate kingdoms—Luang Prabang in the north, Vieng Chan in the center, and Champasak to the south. Each established its own alliances with powerful neighboring states. This stressed the divisions among the three kingdoms and prevented them from reuniting into a strong single kingdom. Between the eighteenth and late-nineteenth centuries, these much-weakened states were riddled by invasions from Burma, Siam, and Annam (Vietnam) as well as by their own internal quarrels and instability.

Angered over foreign intervention and frustrated with the nation's decline, King Chao Anou of Vieng Chan suddenly rebelled against Siamese influence in 1826. The rebellion was short-lived; the Siamese armies captured and razed Vientiane, forcibly resettling thousands of inhabitants on the west bank of the Mekong.

With Vientiane now a vassal of Siam and gangs of Chinese marauders terrorizing the north and the east, the country was ready to fall prey to the hands of colonial powers.

FRENCH RULE

France's early interest in Laos was based on finding a river passage to southern China. French efforts to navigate the Mekong and open up a trade route halted when Khone Falls in the south proved impassable. The French then diverted their interest to exploiting the country's raw materials for their industries at home and in other colonies in Indochina.

By the end of the nineteenth century the French had succeeded in setting up a protectorate in Laos and had reunited its much-reduced borders into a single union. Although the French did little to develop the country and often neglected to involve the Lao in the decision-making process, their rule was, by and large, a mild one. It was under the French, however, that the seeds of an independence movement were sown.

LAOS AND THE SUPERPOWERS

Laos was occupied by the Japanese during World War II. The inability of the French to defend Laos and the eventual surrender of the Japanese in 1945 gave great encouragement to the newly formed Lao Issara (Free Laos) movement. Although the French were to prevail for a few more years, full sovereignty was eventually granted to Laos in 1954.

Prince Souvanna Phouma was the prime minister of Laos in this 1965 photo.

National unity continued to elude the country, however, as it sunk into internal division and involvement in the political problems of its neighbors, particularly Vietnam, which would soon be involved in a major civil war of its own. In the period known as the Cold War, Laos became the focus of global interest. The spread of Communism and the conflicting ideologies of rival superpowers—the Soviet Union, the United States, and China—soon transformed Indochina into a battlefield.

With different political factions vying for power, Laos soon disintegrated into civil war and a rapid succession of coups. The country was split three ways, among the neutralists, who officially represented the royalist government headed by Prince Souvanna Phouma (1901–1984), which believed that a compromise with France was the best way to provide stability to Laos from Communist threats; the right-wing American sympathizers; and the Pathet Lao ("Land of the Lao"), a left-wing resistance movement strongly affiliated with the North Vietnamese Communists.

During the Vietnam War, the North Vietnamese built a secret network of mountain roads and paths through neighboring Laos and Cambodia. They used this route to move troops, weapons, food, and supplies to South Vietnam, where much of the fighting took place. The Vietnamese called the trail Doung Truong Son, *or the Truong Son Road, named for*

the Annamite Mountains (Day Truong Son in Vietnamese). US soldiers nicknamed the route the "Ho Chi Minh Trail" after the Communist revolutionary leader Ho Chi Minh. The name stuck.

The trail was actually a series of tracks, roads, and waterways through the jungle. Some parts were navigable by truck (barely) and others could only accommodate single-file foot traffic. The route also included intricate, interconnecting tunnels with concealed entrances, as well as underground way stations, barracks, radio and telecommunications facilities, and medical aid stations.

Some 43,000 North Vietnamese and Lao—most of whom were forced into service— built or expanded the trail from old, existing mountain paths. In total the trail stretched from north to south about 620 miles (1,000 km), and consisted of many parts. Altogether, the various parts added up to a network of some 9,940 miles (16,000 km) of roads, most of them in Laos.

Under the vast cover of Lao mountain forests, the trail could not be easily seen from the air. The North Vietnamese and Viet Cong (South Vietnamese sympathetic to the North) also used Lao territory because it knew the United States would not enter Laos. In 1962, both North Vietnam and the United States were among the nations that signed the Geneva Accords granting neutral status to Laos. The United States removed its troops from Laos, but the North Vietnamese, for the most part, did not.

The trail was heavily bombed during the war in an effort to disrupt the transport of troops and supplies. However, no matter how much damage was inflicted on the region, the trail was rapidly rebuilt and was never completely destroyed or abandoned.

Today, a new highway runs from Hanoi in the north of Vietnam to Ho Chi Minh City (the former Saigon) in the south. Although it is called the Ho Chi Minh Highway, and commemorates the infamous route, it is located completely in Vietnam.

As the conflict in Vietnam escalated, Vientiane became a center for US undercover operations in the region. North Vietnam's main supply route, the Ho Chi Minh Trail, ran along Laos's eastern border. The Americans carpet bombed the trail, as well as the Pathet Lao stronghold, the Plain of Jars, and other strategic provinces. The United States also deployed a CIA-backed "secret army" in Laos, made up mostly of US-trained Hmong and Thai mercenaries. By the time US troops began pulling out of Vietnam in 1972 and a ceasefire was signed in Paris the following year, more than 750,000 Lao had been forced to flee their homes because of the fighting.

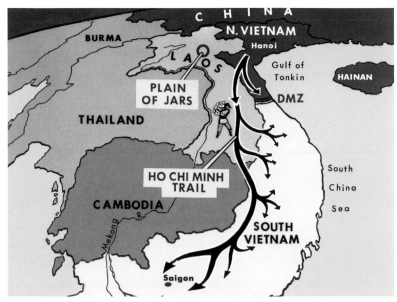

This map shows the rough location of the Ho Chi Minh Trail.

INDEPENDENCE AND BEYOND

With the decisive takeover of the country by the Pathet Lao forces in 1975, more than six hundred years of monarchy came to an abrupt end. The king and his family, along with the royalist military officers and civil servants who had stayed on, were sent to so-called re-education camps (indoctrination prisons) in the north of the country. With the abolition of the monarchy on December 2, 1975, the former Kingdom of Laos, the Land of a Million Elephants, became the Lao People's Democratic Republic.

The new government immediately faced a number of major social and economic problems. The end of US aid coincided with an economic blockade by Thailand. Hundreds of thousands of displaced refugees had to be resettled.

To make matters worse, most of the country's qualified administrators, doctors, and engineers fled Laos. An exodus of businessmen, traders, mechanics, and artisans also ensued. In the ten years following the revolution, more than 10 percent of the population, or three hundred thousand Lao, left the country as refugees.

Laos' civil war ran more or less concurrent with Vietnam's. Its roots can be traced to the end of World War II in 1945 and the return of French occupation in 1946. Both civil wars were complicated by the involvement of superpowers playing out a so-called "proxy war" on their territory. The Cold War antagonists, the United States and the Soviet Union, together with Communist China, used the regional Southeast Asian conflicts to advance their own interests in blocking or expanding communism.

During this time, the North Vietnamese, along with the sympathetic Pathet Lao, occupied parts of Laos, including the Plain of Jars region and the Ho Chi Minh Trail on Laos' eastern border. The US Central Intelligence Agency (CIA) was clandestinely training Lao ethnic minority mountain people (mostly the Hmong) as militia and guerrilla units to resist the communists.

US forces became involved in fighting—mostly aerial bombing—in Laos both to

A pile of used bombs and bomb fragments.

support the royal Lao government in its war against the Pathet Lao and to target North Vietnamese troops. Throughout these years, four different US presidents—Eisenhower, Kennedy, Johnson, and Nixon—did not tell the American people about US covert operations in Laos. In fact, the United States officially denied involvement in what came to be known as the Secret War until 1997. The denial was considered necessary because the United States had acknowledged Laos as a neutral country, and therefore off limits, and because North Vietnam had essentially conquered a large part of Laos, but was denying its involvement as well.

Of course, the Secret War was no secret to the Lao people. From 1964 to 1973, areas of Laos controlled by North Vietnam were subjected to years of intense US aerial bombardment—an average of one attack every eight minutes for nearly ten years—the heaviest bombing campaign in history. When it ended, about one-tenth of the Lao population had been killed.

Agricultural collectives were set up and property belonging to members of the old regime was confiscated. But the farming cooperatives proved economically unmanageable and, in 1979, were abolished and replaced with moderate market socialism. The Soviet Union ended aid to Laos in the late 1980s, and in 1997 Laos joined the Association of Southeast Asian Nations (ASEAN), a regional group that promotes economic cooperation among member countries.

A steady improvement in relations with nonsocialist countries resulted in the resumption of international aid to Laos. Many Buddhist ceremonies and festivals associated with the country's traditional culture have been revived, and peace, stability, and even the prospect of moderate prosperity may finally have returned to Laos.

INTERNET LINKS

https://www.archaeology.org/exclusives/articles/5126-archive-plain-of-jars
Archaeology magazine published this article about the Plain of Jars.

http://www.bbc.com/news/world-asia-pacific-15355605
BBC News provides a timeline of Laotian history beginning in 1893.

http://legaciesofwar.org/about-laos/secret-war-laos
This quick overview of the Secret War focuses on the bombing of Laos and the unexploded ordnances that remain.

http://www.lonelyplanet.com/laos/history
This travel site offers a good overview of the history of Laos.

https://www.si.com/more-sports/2017/06/16/ho-chi-minh-trail-laos-vietnam-war-rebecca-rusch
This moving story in *Sports Illustrated* recounts the journey of an American bicycler down the Ho Chi Minh Trail in memory of her father, who died in Laos in 1972, fighting the Vietnam War.

Prime Minister Thongloun Sisoulit delivers a keynote speech during the ASEAN summit in Vientiane in 2016.

3

"THE LAO PEOPLE'S DEMOCRATIC Republic is an independent country with sovereignty and territorial integrity over its territorial waters and airspace. It is a unified country belonging to all multiethnic people and is indivisible." So states Article 1 of the constitution of the Lao People's Democratic Republic (Sathalanalat Pasathipatai Paxaxon Lao).

The French name for the country, *Laos*, is still commonly used by foreigners and in most books and articles about the country. The Lao themselves refer to their own country as Pathet Lao. *Pathet* means "country" or "land." It is becoming common now among some Western residents and diplomats to refer to the country as Lao, dropping the s, which the French introduced. The Lao people are sometimes called Laotians, but this too is being dropped in favor of "the Lao."

THE CONSTITUTION

Following the 1975 revolution, the government officially became Marxist-Leninist in its political philosophy. Communist rule existed without a written constitution for the first fifteen years. That meant it also proceeded without codified penal and criminal codes.

The first independent constitution of Laos was endorsed in mid-1991 and remains in effect. Internal reforms took place, and several members of the old guard retired. At the same time, it was announced that the

With the introduction of pro-capitalist economic reforms in the early 1990s, the old state emblem, the Russian hammer and sickle and the Vietnamese star, was quietly removed from all official documents and replaced by the silhouette of Pha That Luang, Vientiane's foremost Buddhist temple.

state motto, "Peace, Independence, Unity, and Socialism," would henceforth be "Peace, Independence, Democracy, Unity, and Prosperity."

The constitution legally established a structure of government including the usual executive, legislative and judicial branches at the national level. However, regarding regional governing, the document leaves governors, mayors, and district and village leaders free to "administer their regions and localities without any assistance from popularly elected bodies."

The constitution asserts the equality of men and women as well as the freedom of religion, speech, press, and assembly, though in practice, those liberties are not backed up with legal protections.

ADMINISTERING THE COUNTRY

Article 2 of the constitution states, "The State of the Lao People's Democratic Republic is a people's democratic state. All powers belong to the people, [and are exercised] by the people and for the interests of the multi-ethnic people of all social strata with the workers, farmers and intelligentsia as key components."

Article 3 continues, "The rights of the multi-ethnic people to be the masters of the country are exercised and ensured through the functioning of the political system with the Lao People's Revolutionary Party as its leading nucleus."

With that, the constitution asserts that the central governing body is the Lao People's Revolutionary Party (LPRP). It is the only legal political party in Laos. The LPRP is directed by the party congress, which meets every four to five years to elect new party leaders.

The president is the head of state. The president and vice president are indirectly elected by the National Assembly for a five-year term, with no term limits. In April 2016, Bounnyang Vorachit became the president and Phankham Viphavan became the vice president. The next election is to take place in 2021. The head of government is the prime minister, who is nominated by the president, and elected by the National Assembly for a five-year term. Prime Minister Thongloun Sisoulit was elected in 2016, and will serve until 2021.

The 149-seat National Assembly is the nation's main legislative branch. Lao citizens elect members of the assembly from candidate lists provided by the Lao People's Revolutionary Party. Members serve for five-years.

The judiciary consists of the People's Supreme Court. It is made up of the court president and organized into criminal, civil, administrative, commercial, family, and juvenile chambers, each with a vice president and several judges.

The president appoints provincial governors and mayors. Laos is divided into sixteen provinces, or *khwaeng*. Each province, including Vientiane, which is an independent prefecture, is divided into districts called *muang*. These are further divided into two or more subdistricts or cantons known as *tasseng*, which are made up of villages called *baan*.

The Laotian flag flies above the Presidential Palace in Vientiane.

FOREIGN RELATIONS

Relations between Laos and its neighbors have improved considerably in recent years. Violent border clashes with Thailand in the late 1980s have

The flag of Laos reflects its national colors of red, white, and blue. It consists of three horizontal bands of red (top), blue (double width), and red with a large white disk centered on the blue band. The red stands for the blood shed for liberation, and the blue represents the Mekong River and prosperity. The white disk symbolizes the full moon against the Mekong River, but also signifies the unity of the people under the Lao People's Revolutionary Party, as well as the country's bright future.

The state symbol is the Indian elephant. Historically, Laos was the Land of a Million Elephants. A white elephant was once the symbol of the monarchy.

The national emblem pictures the Pha That Luang shrine, the Nam Ngun hydroelectric dam, a forest, a rice paddy, and a street, a machinery gear, and a rising sun, all framed by stalks of rice. The inscription reads Peace, Independence, Democracy, Unity and Prosperity.

been resolved, though sporadic uprisings by Lao resistance groups based in Thailand continue to test ties. Visits by the Thai royal family and the opening of the Thai-Lao Friendship Bridge in 1994 have gone a long way to ensure that landlocked Laos has both an ally and an open door for trade along its long western frontier.

Relations with China have also thawed following a state visit to Beijing by then-President Kaysone Phomvihan in 1991. Laos is the only country in Indochina to have maintained relations with the United States since the revolution. Ties have strengthened since Laos agreed to cooperate over two key issues: the narcotics trade and the search for the remains of American military personnel missing in action in the rugged Lao terrain. Relations improved further when Laos earned Normal Trade Relations status with the United States in 2004.

When Soviet aid ended, the withdrawal of most of its technical advisers and diplomatic staff made Laos turn more toward Thailand, the West, and Japan, its largest aid donor, for economic assistance. Trading partners Australia, France, and Germany also provide aid. Bilateral relations with Vietnam have remained cordial, but Laos's dependence on its old ally has weakened as it has developed relations with other countries in the region, such as its fellow Association of Southeast Asian Nations (ASEAN) members, and farther afield. The withdrawal of some fifty thousand Vietnamese troops from Laos in 1988 and the 1992 death of President Kaysone Phomvihan, who was half Vietnamese, further weakened the historical links between the two countries.

The Lao government hopes that in the future it will benefit from its role as a bridge between its powerful neighbors without being overwhelmed by them.

INTERNET LINKS

https://www.cia.gov/library/publications/the-world-factbook/geos/la.html
The CIA World Factbook provides up to date information about the government in Laos.

https://www.constituteproject.org/constitution/Laos_2003.pdf?lang=en
This is an English language translation of the Lao constitution.

ECONOMY

The kip (LAK) is the currency of Laos. This ₭2,000 banknote is adorned with a portrait of former President Kaysone Phomvihane.

4

ECONOMICALLY, LAOS IS performing at an impressive rate. The economy's growth has been among the fastest in Asia, averaging nearly 8 percent per year for most of the last decade. Foreign investment in new hydroelectric power projects has been robust, and the growing tourism industry reflects positively in the retail and services trades. In 2013, Laos became a member of the World Trading Organization (WTO), which is not easy to achieve for less developed countries. Doing so means Laos agrees to the WTO's requirements and principles, which is expected to improve its economic climate for the private sector and broaden the country's embrace of a market economy—as opposed to the centrally planned economic model that most communist countries historically favored.

In January 2011, Laos opened a new stock market, the Lao Securities Exchange (LSX), based in Ventiane, as part of a tentative experiment with capitalism.

The entrance way of the Association of Southeast Asian Nations sports the flags of member nations.

That said, Laos remains one of the poorest countries in the world. A huge foreign debt, a lack of skilled workers, and a per capita income of about $5,700 a year paint a bleak picture. The quality of life, however, particularly at the social and cultural level, gives a more positive impression.

Most of the country's self-reliant villages produce sufficient amounts of food to live on and to exchange with neighboring villages. The system of agricultural collectives introduced by the communists proved unpopular and was soon abolished. Most farmers now own their own piece of land.

By 1979 it was clear that Marxist economic policies were not working. With the country tottering on the edge of bankruptcy, the government introduced sweeping reforms. The New Economic Mechanism, or Open Door Policy, was launched in 1986. By the mid-1990s capitalism had started to spread and take root, and its effects were beginning to show, especially in the cities.

The government began by loosening restrictions on private enterprise. State-owned businesses and factories that were not profitable were sold. Inflation has dropped from a runaway 80 percent in 1989 to less than 7 percent in 2006. The nation's gross domestic product has seen healthy growth, for the most part, since then. Lao unit of currency, the kip, has remained stable.

In this progressive economic climate, with Laos' ASEAN membership and resumption of trade with the United States, foreign investors are looking more favorably at the country. The flow of foreign aid into the country is welcome, as it helps balance Laos's loan deficits, at least for the time being.

AGRICULTURE

About 73 percent of the labor force works in agriculture, but the sector contributes only 21 percent to the economy. Less than 10 percent of the country's total land area, however, is exploited for agricultural use. Glutinous

A farmer breaks soil for rice farming with the help of his water buffalo.

rice is the staple food of the Lao. It is grown by lowland wet-rice farmers and dry-rice cultivators who are members of highland ethnic minority groups. Output has steadily increased in recent years, but a good crop heavily depends on weather conditions. Floods, droughts, a long cold spell, or a plague of rats can have devastating effects on the rural economy.

Other important lowland crops include corn, wheat, soybeans, fruits and vegetables, and cotton. Major cash crops produced in the mountain areas are coffee, tobacco, and cardamom. Another important activity in recent years has been livestock breeding, especially cattle and pigs.

Lao rivers provide a large and reliable yield of fish. Experiments in fish breeding have taken place in the massive reservoir that formed when the Nam Ngum Dam was built. If these projects are successful, Laos will be able to export freshwater fish to Thailand in the near future. Many rural people are dependent on the forests to supplement their diets and collect products such as cardamom and damar resin for sale. Increased hunting for food and extensive illegal trade in live animals and animal parts pose threats to the endangered species.

MINERALS

The remoteness of deposits had made mining uneconomical until recently, but with improvements in the transportation network, more of Laos's mineral wealth is being explored. The country's rich mineral resources may prove to be a great asset in the future.

Laos has large deposits of lignite, iron ore, copper, lead, zinc, coal, and gypsum. Many of the areas with deposits have yet to be surveyed extensively. Other largely untapped resources include gemstones and gold. Australian mining company Oxiana is operating the Sepon gold mine. A number of foreign companies are surveying for oil, and many others have been granted mining and exploration rights. However, in the absence of concrete policies, high standards, and strict enforcement, the mining industry may cause harm to the environment. Rivers have been polluted, and rural life has been affected by resettlement, contamination of drinking water, and loss of livestock.

Sand is mined on the banks of the Mekong River.

FORESTRY

About 20 percent of Laos is still covered in primary forest, with a total forest cover of about 40 percent. That figure includes secondary forests, plantations, and bamboo. This is much decreased from 1940, when primary forests covered 70 percent of the country. Deforestation has become a critical issue.

A deforested section of mountainside land in Oudomxay province in northern Laos.

The plant life consists of teak and other valuable, high-quality hardwoods. More than half of the country's export earnings come from logging. Successive bans on excessive logging and a government reforestation program have failed to compensate for the destruction of Lao forests. More than 1,000 square miles (2,590 square km) of mountain forests disappear every year. Land clearing for hydroelectric projects also worsens the problem.

Illegal logging is one of the prime culprits and provincial governors are known to personally profit from the trade. Corruption, lack of trained forest rangers, and porous borders make it relatively easy to smuggle wood out of the country. The activities of illegal loggers continue to reduce the country's canopy of green.

The problem became so dire that in 2016, Prime Minister Thongloun Sisoulith issued a temporary ban on all timber exports—including logs, timber, processed wood, roots, branches, and trees from natural forests. The ban specifies that all types of wood must be turned into finished products before they are exported. Whether the government will be able to enforce the moratorium remains to be seen.

The government of Laos has set the goal of increasing forest cover up to 70 percent by 2020, which it hopes to achieve through reforestation. Of that, more than 1.2 million acres (500,000 hectares) will be commercial tree plantations. So far, trees have been planted on more than 1 million acres (440,000 ha) of land.

THE BATTERY OF SOUTHEAST ASIA

Along with timber, wood processing, and minerals, the export of hydroelectricity to Thailand is one of the country's greatest sources of foreign revenue. Most of this hydroelectricity comes from the Nam Ngum Dam north of Vientiane and the Xeset Dam in southern Laos. The new Nam Theun 2 hydropower station, which began operations in 2010, is the largest such project so far in Laos, and provides electricity for export to energy-deficient Thailand.

Laos currently has forty-six operational hydropower plants with combined generation capacity of 6,444 megawatts (MW) (a megawatt, equal to one million kilowatts, is a unit of measure used in determining the output of power stations) and an annual power output of about 35,000 million kilowatt hours (a kilowatt hour is a measure of electrical energy equivalent to a power consumption of 1,000 watts for 1 hour). Laos hopes to push that capacity to 24,000 MW by 2030, which would mean the country is operating at top hydro potential. There are fifty-four hydropower plants under construction across the country. These have been scheduled to be completed by 2020.

The **Nam Ngum Dam** and hydroelectric power station.

Of these, sixteen hydropower projects use dams to store or divert water for generating electricity. Construction of a second Nam Ngum Dam began in 2011; this project will be much larger than the first, and, in fact, will be the biggest dam in the country.

INDUSTRY AND TRADE

Although the state has expanded the private sector in the hope of producing and manufacturing more goods for domestic use, Laos continues to depend heavily on imports. Foreign aid finances the majority of these imported goods.

The country's leading exports include electricity, timber, wood processing, tin, and the garment industry. Laos's manufacturing base, however, remains small.

Companies largely operate in the tobacco and food processing sectors. Sawmills, companies producing soft drinks, leather, paper, handicrafts, textiles, pottery, brick, and cement, and other small-scale enterprises are prominent too. Thanks to a steady flow of foreign investment into the country, more joint manufacturing ventures are probable. With a largely

Silk is woven by hand in north Laos.

Lang Xang Avenue in central Vientiane, as seen from the city's Patuxai Victory Gate monument.

unskilled labor force of 3.5 million, however, Laos is unlikely to become an industrial giant in the future.

Laos's biggest trading partner, by far, is Thailand. Much trade is also carried on with China and Vietnam. Imports, consisting mainly of oil and other petroleum products, machinery and motor vehicles, food products, and medicines, outweigh exports but the balance of trade is improving.

TRANSPORTATION

One of the major contributors to the country's economic development is the improvement and extension of its road network. There are about 24,600 miles (39,586 km) of roads in Laos including national highways, provincial roads, local roads, and *routes coloniales* constructed by the French. However, only 3,365 miles (5,415 km) are paved. Route 13, running from Luang Prabang in the north to Vientiane, Savannakhet, Pakse, and the Cambodian border in the south, is the country's longest road. Other routes run east from this main artery and cross over the high mountain passes of the Annamese Cordillera into Vietnam.

FRIENDSHIP BRIDGES

Nothing symbolizes the economic awakening of the country better than the First Friendship Bridge. The bridge, which was officially inaugurated on April 8, 1994, was the country's first major ground transportation link to the world outside.

The bridge connects Tha Nalaeng, near Vientiane, with the Thai town of Nong Khai and is the first such construction to span the Mekong. The bridge, which is 0.7 miles (1.1 km) long, was financed with $30 million of Australian aid. The opening of the bridge was attended by a number of important

The Third Thai-Lao Friendship Bridge gracefully traverses the Mekong River.

people, including the Thai and Australian prime ministers, the Lao president, and King Bhumibol of Thailand.

The Second Friendship Bridge across the Mekong opened in 2006, between Savannakhet and the Thai town of Mudahan. The Third Thai-Lao Friendship Bridge, between Thakhet, Khammouane, in Laos and Nakhon Phanom Province in Thailand, opened in 2011, and the Fourth Thai—Lao Friendship Bridge, between Ban Houayxay in Laos and Chiang Khong district of Thailand, opened in 2013.

That bridge marked the completion of the final section of Asian Highway 3. Asian Highway 3 (AH3) is a route of the Asian Highway Network which runs 4,555 miles (7,331 km) from Ulan-Ude, Russia (AH6) to Tanggu, China; and Shanghai, China (on AH5) to Chiang Rai, Thailand, and Kengtung, Myanmar (both on AH2). In Laos, it includes Route 13 and Route 3, which crosses the Fourth Thai—Lao Friendship Bridge.

A row of bungalows along the Nam Song River houses tourists and trekkers in Vang Vieng.

TOURISM

Laos has become one of the most popular ecotourism destinations of recent years. In the 1960s few visitors traveled far beyond Vientiane and the old royal city of Luang Prabang. The war in Indochina led to a complete suspension of tourism. The country finally opened its doors to visitors in 1989 but with conditions. Since then tourist visits have increased by leaps and bounds. More than 1 million visitors entered Laos in 2005, and ten years later, in 2015, that number had grown to 4.7 million. The Laos Department of Tourism predicts nearly 7.6 million visitors will come to Laos in 2025.

In recent years government support and collaboration with international organizations have improved urban infrastructures and tourist facilities a great deal. The government is worried, however, that allowing too many visitors will have an adverse impact on Laos's culture and way of life. Therefore it prefers to promote what it calls cultural tourism rather than mass tourism. Nonetheless, the country's rich history and culture, colonial buildings and Buddhist temples, magnificent natural scenery, and distinctive highland ethnic minorities are certain to attract more tourists in the future.

Tourists row kayaks along the Nam Song River in Vang Vieng, a popular destination for wilderness adventurers.

INTERNET LINKS

http://www.loc.gov/law/foreign-news/article/laos-illegal-timber-exports
The Library of Congress Law Library provides this report on illegal timber exports in Laos.

http://www.rfa.org/english/news/laos/new-lao-prime-minister-issues-ban-on-timber-exports-05172016152448.html
Radio Free Asia offers this article on Laos' timber export ban and links to related articles.

http://thailand.embassy.gov.au/bkok/FunRun_Bridge_History.html
The Australian Embassy provides a history of the First Thai-Laos Friendship Bridge.

http://www.tourismlaos.org
Laos' official tourism site includes its attractions and figures on the growth of the industry.

ENVIRONMENT

Highway 13 ("the bandit road") hugs the slopes of the Kasi Mountains.

5

BEING RELATIVELY UNDEVELOPED, Laos has less than the usual amount of pollution and other environmental problems that plague more industrialized nations. Landlocked Laos boasts of a wealth of natural resources. Its rugged terrain, limited industrial development, and low population density have nourished acres of flora and fauna. New plants and animals are being discovered. Some species that were once considered extinct have been sighted within its borders. Laos's National Protected Areas (NPAs) are important conservation sites. However, the fate of all its wildlife communities depends on how Laos resolves the conflict among development, resource exploitation, and environmental protection.

Deforestation, cross-border wildlife trade, dam construction, mining, commercial plantations, and urbanization threaten to sap the country's rich biodiversity. Environmental management in Laos has been

One of the greatest environmental problems in Laos is that of unexploded ordnance, or bombs, hidden in the ground. In just ten days of bombing Laos during the Vietnam War, the United States spent $130 million (in 2013 dollars), or more than it spent in over twenty years of cleaning up those bombs. In 2016, President Barack Obama visited Laos and pledged another $90 million to find unexploded bombs and to help victims with medical expenses.

hampered by a lack of equipment, funds, and skilled personnel. The remoteness of many areas complicates conservation efforts, while erratic law enforcement breeds illegal logging and encourages timber smuggling.

SHRINKING BIODIVERSITY

When Laos gained independence from France in the 1940s, its numerous forests were a wildlife haven for many plant and animal species. The International Union for Conservation of Nature and Natural Resources (IUCN) estimated that primary (old-growth) forests dominated half of the country's woodlands then. Today the figure has shrunk to a mere 9 percent. Because lush vegetation supports teeming wildlife, the animal population falls when the forest cover recedes and precious habitats are destroyed.

An Asian golden weaver perches on a branch.

In recent years there has been an upwardly spiraling demand for exotic cuisine (such as scaled anteaters, mouse deer, and squirrels), medicinal cures (such as bears' paws and snakes, birds, and insects bottled in alcohol), and accessories (animal teeth sold as necklaces, framed butterflies and beetles), further decimating their numbers. An increase in the use of firearms for poaching threatens the very survival of countless species of animals.

More than four hundred bird varieties make Laos their home. In the 1990s, British ornithologists recorded eight globally threatened and twenty-one near-threatened species, including the Asian gold weaver, the giant ibis, and the red-collared woodpecker. Unfortunately they are not the only ones dying out. Even the common sparrows are being threatened. The Buddhist practice of gaining merits by releasing caged birds into the open is being discouraged, as these birds often perish shortly after their release, being unable to survive in the wild.

ENDANGERED SPECIES

Certain wildlife previously thought of as extinct has reappeared in Laos in the past few decades. Written about in fourteenth-century Chinese journals, the spindlehorn, or saola, was sighted in the Annamese Cordillera in 1992. The rediscovery of the mammal, which looks like a large white-and-brown deer, along the Lao-Vietnamese border generated much excitement. Unfortunately the spindlehorn remains endangered, as its horns are a hunter's favored trophy.

The Indochinese warty pig is another creature that was previously thought to be lost forever. In 1892 a Jesuit priest purchased some of its skulls in southern Vietnam. The species was not seen again until it recently resurfaced in Nakai-Nam Theum, the largest national protected area in Laos. The prehistoric Laotian rock rat, kha-nyou, believed to have gone extinct eleven million years ago, was found among the lime rocks in Khammoun Province.

DEFORESTATION

For centuries Laos's most valuable resource has been its forests. In 1940 they blanketed 70 percent of the country, but widespread deforestation reduced the woodlands to only 40 percent of the total land area by 2011. Despite passing laws on forestry management, land use, and resource protection, the government appears to have had little impact on logging and timber smuggling. Lao forests continue to vanish at an alarming rate.

Commercial logging is one of the biggest culprits. Timber is a major revenue earner for Laos. In 2005 a significant amount of timber was exported to various markets. Though there has been a drop from the all-time high of 25,920,965 cubic feet (734,000 cubic m) in 1999, organizations still continue to profit at the environment's expense. In 2012, the Environmental Investigation Agency (EIA) estimated that around 17,657,333 cubic feet (500,000 cubic m) of logs made their way from Laos to Vietnam annually with logs coming from "some of the last intact tropical forests in the Mekong region."

A truck loaded with logs from an ancient forest rumbles through the town of Nakai.

In return for building roads, the government allows Chinese businesses to take as much timber as they want from northern Laos. The national electricity company hacks ever-wider tracts along the highways each time it links a town or a village to the power grid. The army clears huge swathes of forests and benefits from timber sales to Vietnam. In fact, the Vietnamese army itself is a major participant in the smuggling of illegally logged timber out of Laos.

Land clearing for agriculture, population growth, hydroelectric dam construction, mining, roads, and other developments have accelerated deforestation. The rapid loss of plant canopy results in soil erosion. Silt accumulates in rivers and irrigation channels, thus polluting water resources and threatening aquatic ecosystems.

The government wants to preserve the country's environment, but lacks the resources to do so effectively. A lack of environmental planning, surveys, and legislation obstruct much real progress, but the government has issued decrees to encourage environmental protection. These decrees indicate a general resolve for protecting forestland—and include prohibitions on cutting certain tree species; regulations on hunting, fishing, and the use of fire during the dry season; and regulations on the management and protection of forestland, wildlife, and fish. However, without effective enforcement, these decrees don't accomplish much.

PROTECTED AREAS

Laos has twenty National Protected Areas (NPA) that covers almost 14 percent of the country. All were established in the 1990s. These reserve areas include vast zones of tropical monsoon forest, diverse wildlife and fascinating karst limestone formations. Many are in southern Laos, where natural forest cover is abundant. Nine have functioning field offices to care for plant and animal life. Some, but not all, protected areas are accessible to the public.

The most accessible parks are the Nam Ha NPA in Louang Namtha, the Nakai-Nam Theum NPA near the Vietnamese border, and the Phu Hin Bun NPA, which includes the Khammouan limestone caves, east of Thakhek. The best time for visitors to view wildlife in these NPAs is in November, just after the monsoon season.

Unlike most other preservation areas, which forbid commercial activities, the Lao NPAs include production forests for timber, protection forests for hydropower watersheds, and conservation forests. There are plans to increase forest cover to 65,637 square miles (17 million ha), or 60 percent of total land area, by 2020. While the merits of a zoning strategy are clear, implementing such activities remains a challenge. The government's conservation commitments are also undercut by the logging and mining concessions it periodically issues within the NPAs.

People explore a cave accessible only by water.

DAM OPPOSITION

The Mekong River sustains freshwater ecosystems as it travels the length of Laos. However, a flurry of dam construction activities are altering the natural environment and erasing traditional lifestyles in their wake. The government acknowledges the disruptive impact of damming but insists that the long-term economic advantages will outweigh the short-term negative effects.

Many experts warn that dams interfere with river flow, thereby destroying water quality. A changing water table of higher- or lower-than-normal fluctuations hinders the ability of certain fish to migrate and spawn upriver. Important fish breeding sites are submerged, and valuable ecologies are destroyed. Farmlands are flooded, wreaking havoc on the communities

NAM NGUM DAM

The Nam Ngum Dam was opened in 1971 with the help of funds and expertise supplied by the United Nations and the United States. It was the first hydroelectric dam in Laos, and was built on the Nam Ngum River, a major tributary of the Mekong. The dam controls flooding along the Mekong and its tributaries. Its power plant generates electricity not just for domestic use but also for export to neighboring Thailand, thus supplying a good third of Laos's foreign earnings.

The Lao are very proud of the dam. Pictures of Nam Ngum Dam and its lake are featured on postcards and tourist brochures. The lake is dotted with dozens of

small islands. Divers using underwater chain saws have logged valuable trees that were overlooked before the valley was flooded.

they support. Fishermen and villagers depending on fish as their main food staple are forced to relocate due to a decline of their numbers. Entire groups and their traditional way of life are lost.

Others argue that the cultural and environmental cost of damming is offset because hydropower is a clean and renewable energy source. Unlike with fossil fuels, the process whereby hydroelectricity is derived does not pollute the air. Controlled irrigation enriches previously infertile soil and prepares new land for crop cultivation. Controlled flooding eliminates erratic flows and rapids, making it easier to navigate the Lao network of rivers.

Despite the controversy, government support for dam construction is strong. Lao officials believe that harnessing hydropower will reduce the nation's dependence on timber. Most important, hydropower could generate millions of dollars for a country where almost three-quarters of the population is in poverty.

THE LINGERING LEGACY OF WAR

Laos is the most heavily bombed place on earth. Between 1964 and 1973, during the American "Secret War," US aircraft flew 580,000 bombing missions over Laos, one of the most intensive air campaigns in the history of warfare. By the time the campaign ended in 1973, a tenth of Laos's population had been killed. US forces dropped 2.2 million tons (2 million metric tons) of explosives on the country, including 277 million cluster bombs. Of those, some 80 million failed to explode.

A cluster bomb is a container filled with small explosive bombs called submunitions or bomblets. Some contain hundreds of bomblets. Dropped from an aircraft or fired from the ground, a cluster bomb opens in the air and releases its deadly cargo, scattering a carpet of bombs indiscriminately over a large area.

Many decades after the end of that war, unexploded ordnance remains a serious environmental problem for Laos. The ground is contaminated with hidden live munitions, buried in the soil, sunken in rice paddies and riverbeds,

A woman walks past rusted hulks of cluster bomb shells in a scrap metal shop in Phonsavanh.

For the Lao who live in Xieng Khuang, even war debris has its uses. Materials left over from the last Indochina war have been recycled into useful commodities. A brisk trade in recycled war scrap has grown over the years, with flare casings, bombshells, and pieces of airplane fuselages being collected and hoarded and then sold to scrap metal merchants. These are melted down and resold for commercial use.

War debris that is not sold is often stored by residents in the space under their stilted houses and then used when they can come up with a recycling plan for it. Many shell casings serve as fences, cattle troughs, water vessels, pillars to support houses and barns, and planters for growing vegetables. In one village a B-52 shell casing hangs from a frame at the side of the road, serving as a fire bell. Some bomb craters have been improvised into harmless service as fish and duck ponds. Lotuses can often be seen blooming on the surface of these artificial ponds. There are many examples of such resourceful use of war waste.

and embedded in trees. In 2014 alone, some 56,400 munitions were found and destroyed, but many are not found until it's too late. Some of the corroded bombs look like stones. Many a farmer working in a field has set one off after hitting it with his hoe.

Non-corroded ones are sometimes brightly colored, a characteristic which unintentionally attracts children at play. Since the war's end, more than eight thousand people have been killed and about twelve thousand injured by cluster bombs and other leftover explosives there. Almost half of the victims were children under sixteen.

Each year, the United States gives money to Laos to fund the removal of these unexploded bombs. In 2016, President Barack Obama visited Laos and promised to double US aid to Laos for that purpose to $30 million a year for three years. This figure is a great increase over the annual US contribution of

$2.5 million a decade before. Those funds account for only 30 percent of the monies being contributed internationally to this effort, from organizations and nations, including Australia, Ireland, Japan, Norway and Switzerland. Even so, progress is slow, and it will be decades before all the unexploded bombs are removed from the Laotian countryside.

In 2008, about one hundred countries met in Ireland and negotiated a ban on cluster bombs. Russia, China, and the United States did not take part.

INTERNET LINKS

http://factsanddetails.com/southeast-asia/Laos/sub5_3d/ entry-2975.html
http://factsanddetails.com/southeast-asia/Laos/sub5_3d/ entry-2983.html
These sites provides excerpts from other sources in bulleted lists of topics relating to environment, energy, hydropower, dams, and unexploded ordnance in Laos.

https://www.nytimes.com/2015/04/06/world/asia/laos-campaign-to-clear-millions-of-unexploded-bombs.html?mcubz=0
This article focuses on one woman's campaign to attract attention to the problem of unexploded bombs in Laos.

https://www.nytimes.com/2017/06/05/science/animal-farms-southeast-asia-endangered-animals.html
The illegal trade in endangered animals is the subject of this article.

http://www.trekkingcentrallaos.com/html/nationalpark.html
This site highlights the Phou Khao Khouay National Protected Area.

https://visitlaos.org/national-parks
This travel site discusses Laos' national protected areas.

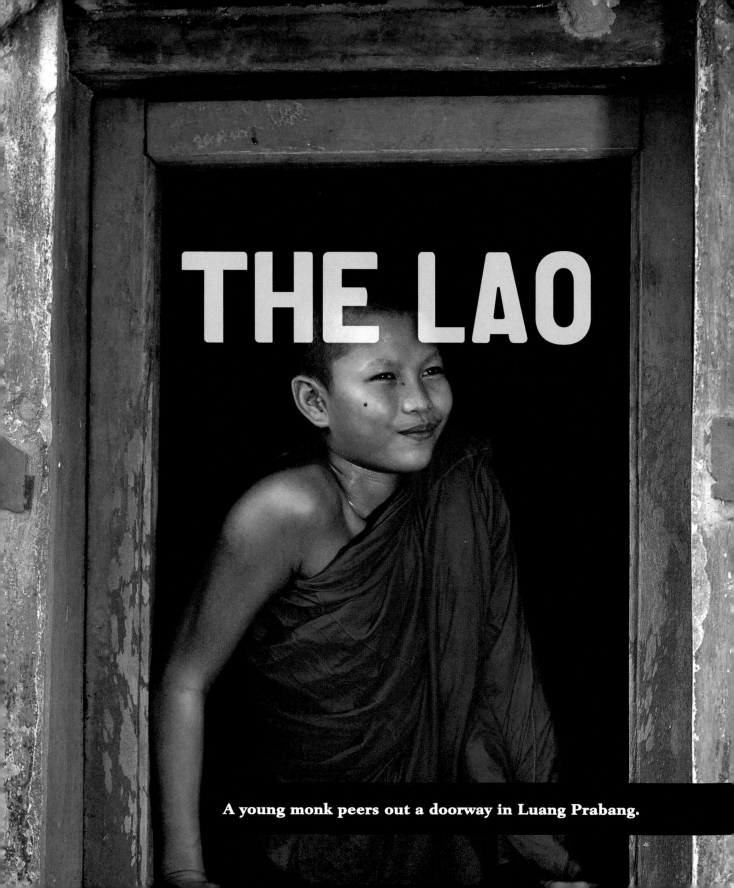

THE LAO

A young monk peers out a doorway in Luang Prabang.

6

The Lao government officially recognizes forty-nine ethnic groups, but the total number of ethnic groups is thought to be well over two hundred.

THE PEOPLE OF LAOS ARE CALLED the Lao. Confusingly, however, not all of the Lao are Lao. That is, the term is a description of both national and ethnic identity. It applies to the Lao ethnic group, which makes up the majority of the country's population—about 53 percent—but not all of it. In English, the word *Laotian* is also correct as a noun—the name of the people; and as an adjective—describing things relating to the people or the country. The word derives from the French *Laotien/Laotienne*, but seems to be losing ground in common usage to the term *Lao*.

The demographic makeup of the national population is uncertain because the government divides the people into three groups according to the altitude at which they live, rather than according to ethnic origin. Accordingly, the lowland Lao (Lao Loum) account for 68 percent of the population; upland Lao (Lao Theung) for 22 percent; and the highland Lao (Lao Soung, including the Hmong and the Yao) for 9 percent.

Ethnic Vietnamese people comprise about 2 percent of the population. However, alternative ways of sorting the population into ethnic categories result in different statistics.

DEMOGRAPHIC OVERVIEW

The estimated population of Laos in 2017 was 7.1 million people. In comparison with other Asian countries, Laos is sparsely inhabited, with a population density of about 73 inhabitants per square mile (28 per square km). The government is encouraging population growth. Improvements in health and sanitation have helped to reduce the high infant mortality rate, and children under the age of fifteen now make up about one third of the population. At about 64.3 years, however, average life expectancy at birth remains very low.

More than two-thirds of the population live in the rural provinces, although a steady urbanization is taking place. The most populated provinces are Savannakhet, (969,700), Vientiane municipality (783,000), and Champasak (694,000).

A Lao Loum woman holds her child outside her bamboo hut in the village of San By My in northwestern Laos.

Historically Southeast Asia has been a melting pot of races, cultures, and religions. Laos has the highest number of minorities in the region. The Lao Loum, the country's earliest settlers, are the majority.

There are four main ethnolinguistic groups. The Lao Loum are known for being the country's lowlanders; the Lao Tai dwell in the upland valleys; the Lao Theung occupy the mountain slopes and river valleys; and the Lao Soung, the country's highland dwellers, generally live at altitudes of more than 3,000 feet (914 m).

THE LAO LOUM

The Lao are a subgroup of the Tai peoples who once occupied Yunnan Province in southern China. They learned about wet-rice farming and martial arts. This helped them to settle and gain mastery over the Mekong floodplains and to force other groups up into the higher areas. Today most city and town residents are Lao Loum.

The Lao Loum, who refer to themselves simply as Lao, are the country's dominant racial group. They are the architects of most of the nation's main traditions and institutions.

The official language of the country, Lao, is the dialect spoken by these lowland people. The Lao language belongs to the Tai sublanguage family, which falls under the Tai-Kadai language family. The state religion, Theravada Buddhism, is the faith of the Lao Loum.

An old woman wears a traditional ethnic national costume.

THE LAO TAI

The Lao Tai, who mostly inhabit the mountain valleys of northern Laos, are closely related to the Lao Loum. They subsist as farmers growing wet rice, millet, corn, sweet potatoes, and beans as well as dry rice and wheat on mountain slopes.

Unlike the Lao Loum, the Lao Tai have generally maintained their animist beliefs and will go to great lengths to appease malevolent spirits. The Lao Tai distinguish themselves by the color of their clothing (Black Tai and Red Tai) or by the general areas they inhabit (the Forest Tai and the Northern Tai). The Lao government considers the Lao Tai to be part of the Lao Loum group.

THE LAO THEUNG

The Lao Theung are believed to be the original inhabitants of Laos. They are an Austro-Asiatic group who reside around the middle altitudes of mountain slopes. About 22 percent of the population belongs to the Lao Theung, the second-largest group in the country.

Their language belongs to the Mon-Khmer language family. Large numbers of Lao Theung are found in the north and south of the country. Traditionally

A woman of the Lao Theung ethnic group lives on a mountain in the north of Laos.

the Lao Theung lived a seminomadic existence as hunters and slash-and-burn farmers. Many have now settled on the land and cultivate crops such as rice, corn, cotton, tobacco, coffee, and tea. They usually trade with other groups by bartering supplies.

The Lao Theung often live with their extended families in large wooden longhouses built on piles. Made from bamboo, timber, and woven cane, the buildings are spacious and usually have high roofs. Some Lao Theung have adopted Buddhism. Others have remained animists.

Their place in Lao society has often been lower than that of other groups. They were known in former times as the Kha, or "slaves." Members of Lao Theung groups such as the Khamu, the Lamet, and the Lawa (also called the Htin) worked as court servants before the 1975 revolution. Even today, many Lao Theung work in poorly paid manual jobs for the wealthier lowland Lao.

THE LAO SOUNG

The Lao Soung, who represent less than 10 percent of the population, are the most recent arrivals in Laos. Their migration from China occurred only in the past 250 years. They are the most ethnically distinct of all the groups. Known in Laos as the Chinese group, the main subgroups are the Hmong, the Akha, the Yao, the Mien, the Ho, and the Laho.

The language of the Lao Soung belongs to the Tibeto-Burman family. The Lao Soung practice indigenous Tai folk religions called Satsana Phi ("religion of spirits"), which include animist traditions. Elements of ancestor worship, Buddhism, and even Confucianism surface in their religious rituals, ceremonies, and feasts.

These highlanders consider themselves superior to the lowland Lao. This has often led to differences between the two groups. The Lao Soung are a fiercely independent people. Following the 1975 revolution many, especially the Hmong, fled abroad to escape persecution for fighting against the Communists. Many of those who remained in Laos were forcibly relocated from their mountain homes. Large numbers of Lao Soung are found in Myanmar, Vietnam, China, and Thailand.

Many of the Lao Soung are shifting cultivators, but they also live in settled communities. Villagers grow corn, cassava, mountain rice, tapioca, sugarcane, and root vegetables such as yams. They also breed animals, including water buffaloes and horses.

The Lao Soung are known for their excellent manual skills. Many of the groups produce tools, as well as silver ornaments and textiles.

The high ground occupied by the Hmong is also perfect for growing poppies, the raw material from which opium is made. This has been an embarrassment to the Lao government, which has largely succeeded in putting an end to the production of this cash crop by destroying fields and resettling the villagers.

A Hmong woman wears festive traditional clothing in Xiangkhouang.

OTHER COMMUNITIES

The Chinese are one of the largest foreign communities in Laos, as they are in most other countries in Southeast Asia. The majority of Chinese residents live in the cities of Vientiane and Savannakhet. They work as traders or run their own businesses. Many shops, hotels, and cinemas in Laos are owned by ethnic Chinese.

Another important minority are the Vietnamese. The French and later the North Vietnamese government encouraged their settlement. They engage

The apparel of the Lao highland ethnic minorities, particularly the clothes worn by women, helps to distinguish one ethnic group from another. In some cases, the name of a group can be guessed from its color and design preferences. For example, the main Hmong groups are described as Black, Blue, White, and Striped Hmong according to the color and type of their women's attire.

Styles vary greatly among the groups. The Hmong are known for embroidered designs, strips of colorful appliqué, and dyed pleated skirts. The Yao are noted for baggy trousers, long tunics, bright red ruffs, and the pompoms that their children wear. The Lanten, a little-known minority, are distinguished by their white leggings and indigo trousers, as well as by the shaved eyebrows of their women. The Akha are characterized by close-fitting headdresses decorated with coins, bright metal disks, shells, and beads.

Silver is regarded by the highland peoples as a source of wealth, almost like money in the bank. Silver pendants, chains, rings, bracelets, and breastplates are dazzling when worn against black, red, and indigo cloth. Some groups use old silver coins as earrings or necklaces or to decorate the borders of headdresses and skirt hems. Many are old French colonial coins; others come from China and Thailand. Old Burmese and Indian rupee coins from the days of the British Empire are found occasionally. Silver buttons beaten from coins are also considered important decorations.

It is not surprising that the strong visual appeal of the highland people's fashions have influenced Western designers.

in similar trades as the Chinese but tend to live in border and rural areas. There are a small number of Khmer (aboriginal Cambodians) living in the southern province of Champasak. They can be found in the trade and transportation industries.

With improved relations between Thailand and Laos, an increasing number of Thai are taking up temporary residence as businesspeople or education and aid workers. A small number of Indians, Pakistanis, and Bangladeshis have also made Vientiane their home. They are mostly shopkeepers, tailors, and tradesmen. Some of them can be seen selling fabrics and cloth every day at the large morning market.

These days a small but growing number of Europeans, Australians, Americans, and Japanese can be found living and working in Laos. Many of those who are not running businesses often work for organizations such as the United Nations, the World Health Organization (WHO), or one of the many nongovernmental organizations such as the Red Cross.

INTERNET LINKS

https://www.britannica.com/place/Laos#toc52500
The encyclopedia entry for Laos includes a section on the country's ethnic groups.

http://www.hilltribe.org/hmong/hmong-dress.php
This site describes traditional dress among some Hmong groups with photos.

https://www.luangprabang-laos.com/Home/Lao-Country/The-people-tribes-and-ethnical.html
This travel site provides an overview of the different Lao ethnic groups.

https://theartofhmongembroidery.wordpress.com/tag/traditional-hmong-clothes
Many styles of Hmong traditional clothing are shown on this site.

LIFESTYLE

A man waters a field of vegetables growing along the Nam Ngum River.

Except for the occasional bad year, crops are regular and consistent. This perhaps explains the general sense of satisfaction that prevails among most rural Lao. For the farmers of the dry mountainous regions such as those in northern Laos, circumstances are different. Variations in the weather and the poorer quality of soil give them less reason to feel secure.

A farmer soaks rice seedlings in water and mud to prepare them for planting.

URBAN LIFE

Laos is the least urbanized country in Indochina. There are no cities to compare, in size or atmosphere, with the likes of Phnom Penh in Cambodia or Hanoi in Vietnam. The capital, Vientiane, is the only Lao settlement that remotely resembles a city, although Savannakhet is a developed commercial center, and Luang Prabang remains an important cultural hub.

Part of Vientiane's charm has always been its laidback personality. Its tree-lined avenues, crumbling old French villas, and riverside bars and cafés are reminders of a different age that remain untouched by the frantic rush of modern life. Some of that appeal has vanished with greater prosperity, the arrival of foreign investors and aid workers, and the influence of nearby Thailand. Discos, branded goods, Western clothes, and Thai television and pop music are now part of the Vientiane scene, for better or worse.

EDUCATION

Traditionally the education system in Laos was run by monks. Classes were held in the courtyard of the local pagoda. With the arrival of the French, secular schools were introduced and the French language taught. Some schools in Laos are still attached to monasteries, although the teachers are not limited to the monks.

The LPRP—the Lao People's Revolutionary Party—began a policy aimed at providing basic education for all children and eradicating illiteracy among the adult population. Although Laos's literacy levels remain low in comparison with those of neighboring countries such as Vietnam and Thailand, they are slowly improving.

Children of the Akha Ya-Er hill tribe enjoy their lessons at the local primary school.

Education is compulsory for all children between seven and fifteen years old, but this is not always possible to enforce, especially in remote rural areas or among the seminomadic highland people. In some places, the problem is a lack of access. Of the 10,553 villages country-wide, only 45 percent have schools that go up to grade 3, and 20 percent of communities have no schools at all. For others, it may be a language barrier, as school is taught in Lao, a language they may not speak at home. Primary education begins at age seven. Secondary education starts at age eleven and lasts for seven years—an extra year was added in 2010 to bring the total to twelve)—but many students drop out before completion.

There are also more male than female students. Like others in Southeast Asia, many Lao families have traditionally believed it's more important for sons to be educated than for daughters. About 87 percent of men can read and write compared with just 73 percent of women, but these numbers are rising as both genders of the younger generation attend school equally. Between 2009 and 2011, primary school enrollment increased from 91.6 percent to

Young students focus on their school work in a class in Savannakhet.

97 percent. However, the number of children who drop out of school before completing grade 5 is still quite high, and many girls, particularly in rural areas, will stay home to care for younger siblings.

Founded in 1996, the National University of Laos is the only university in the country. Located in Vientiane, its nine colleges offer subjects ranging from forestry and agriculture to teaching and communications. During the 1970s and 1980s, many students were sent to the Soviet Union or Vietnam for higher education. This practice has stopped, but other things remain the same, including low pay for teachers and limited funds for textbooks and other educational materials.

HEALTH

Homemade traditional medicine ferments in a bottle.

Despite great strides in building up the economy in the past few years, the country's health standards and medical care remain woefully inadequate. This is reflected in its relatively high infant-mortality rate. About 51.4 out of every 1,000 Lao babies die in their first year of life due to malnutrition, diseases, and lack of access to proper medical facilities. About 197 women per 100,000 die of pregnancy or birth-related complications. These statistics, called the infant mortality and maternal mortality rates, are averages, and vary across the country's different regions. Sekong province, for example, one of the poorest areas, has an infant mortality rate of 70 per 1,000 live births and maternal mortality ratio of 357 per 100,000 live births according to 2015 statistics from the provincial health office. And about 26.5 percent of children under age five are underweight, on average.

Public health care is concentrated in the cities, especially Vientiane, and is virtually nonexistent in remote areas. There is also a shortage of medical staff, with fewer than 1,300 doctors spread across the country. The health care system was greatly damaged by the mass departure of many skilled doctors and other medical workers after the Pathet Lao's 1975 takeover, and it remains weak. Despite assistance from foreign organizations there is still a chronic lack of basic medicine, essential equipment, and experienced personnel.

In the countryside the widespread belief in the supernatural origins of illness has hindered some health programs, especially the immunization of children.

WOMEN

The division of labor between the sexes in rural areas is almost as rigid now as it was generations ago. Men plow the fields, hunt, fish, build boats, fell trees, make basic tools, repair fences, and pursue other, similar tasks.

Women's work, if anything, is even more difficult. Women are responsible for running the household and bringing up children. In addition they are expected to cook, clean, spin and weave, carry wood, and tend the kitchen garden and are responsible for the backbreaking task of carrying and fetching water. They are also obliged to hull rice by pounding it in a large mortar with

A woman carries pails to retrieve water for the family.

a heavy pestle. Women play an important part in economic activities outside the home as well. Most of the bartering and selling of produce in the markets are done by women.

Many women fought alongside men in the country's struggle for independence. Although women are now more highly educated than they were before the 1975 revolution, few real measures have been taken to improve the traditionally subordinate position of women in Lao society. In sharp contrast to Vietnam, where women have been encouraged to develop leadership skills, in Laos women have played a relatively minor role in its history. Politics remains an almost exclusive male domain, with very few women in senior positions in the government.

MARRIAGE

Arranged marriages are no longer common in Laos. Although the choice of a life partner is usually a personal matter, the heads of both families are consulted in advance of the wedding. The steps leading to marriage are complex. A formal request for the hand of the bride is usually made in the presence of a village elder or a monk.

Lao models pose in traditional wedding costumes.

Both families usually consult an astrologer to make sure that the couple's birthdays and fates are well matched. It is the parents who decide when the couple will marry, where they will live, and the sum to be paid as a bride price, or *kha dong* (kaa DONG). This is delivered to the bride's father on the wedding eve, when the groom's family will turn up at the bride's house with gifts of food, betel nuts, and other offerings.

Couples are married by village elders or a local monk in a simple Buddhist ceremony, which requires no exchange of rings. Traditional Lao dress is worn by both the bride and the groom; a *baci sukhwan* (BAH-see sukhwan), a distinctive Lao ceremony, is held, and sumptuous food is served at the reception. It is considered lucky to entertain strangers during the ceremony.

BIRTH AND ADULTHOOD

The naming ceremony of a newborn child is the first big event in a Lao's life. A *baci*, or ritual, in which money is attached to the infant's arms is held for family members, friends, and neighbors and sometimes for the entire population of a village. The size of the feast depends on the wealth of the family. A *bonze*, or Buddhist monk, is asked to choose a name for the child, one that will depend on the astrological specifications at the time of the child's birth.

For a boy, the next most important ceremony is one that marks his transition from childhood to adulthood. The manhood ceremony usually takes place around the age of thirteen. Only close relatives are invited to this ritual, which involves cutting off the boy's hair. In more traditional areas,

A mother bathes her baby boy in the remote Khmu village of Ban Kengdeung in Phongsaly Province.

boys still sometimes receive a tattoo as a symbol of manhood. This has the added value of warding off evil spirits.

DEATH

The final and most important ceremony for a Lao is the funeral. The ministrations of bonzes at funerals are mandatory and more marked than for birth or marriage. They are involved in almost every stage of the elaborate ceremonies up to the final cremation.

After the body has been prepared, it is placed in a coffin, and private family rituals are held. Expressions of grief are kept to a minimum. The Lao firmly believe that displays of sadness retard the rebirth of the spirit of the deceased into a better existence and block him from attaining the final goal of nirvana, or transcendence of suffering and desire.

A Buddhist funeral takes place in a village near Luang Prabang.

After the family rites, the body is placed in a shelter in the garden or the yard, and a series of feasts and ceremonies begins. The body is finally taken to a cremation pyre on a riverbank or in a field. It is washed, exposed to the sky, and then cremated. Sometimes relatives burn jewelry with the deceased. The one who finds burnt gold while collecting the ashes is considered blessed, and it is said that the deceased wanted him or her to have it. The ashes are then kept in a small stupa at the village *wat* (WHAT), or temple.

Families who cannot afford these elaborate rituals resort to a simple burial in the forest. Graves are left unmarked in such cases, and it is hoped that all traces of the burial spot will vanish as quickly as possible; otherwise the spirit of the dead runs the risk of being influenced by malevolent spirits, which in remote areas are believed to harass villages and travelers.

INTERNET LINKS

http://factsanddetails.com/southeast-asia/Laos/sub5_3b/entry-2954.html
Family life in Laos, along with the roles of men, women, and children are discussed on this page.

http://factsanddetails.com/southeast-asia/Laos/sub5_3d/entry-2982.html
This site offers many facts about health and health care issues in Laos.

http://www.laos-guide-999.com/Laos-wedding.html
A detailed description of a typical Lao wedding ceremony is given on this site.

http://luangnamthaguide.com/2011/04/a-lao-funeral
This page describes a Lao funeral ceremony, with many photos.

RELIGION

A huge, golden reclining Buddha statue is an impressive sight in a park near the Great Golden Stupa in Vientiane.

8

BUDDHISM, THE DOMINANT religion of Laos, is based on the teachings of the Buddha ("the Awakened One"). He was born Siddhartha Gautama, the son of a Nepalese prince who lived more than 2,500 years ago in what is now Nepal. Buddha himself was not and never claimed to be a god, but rather a teacher.

Theravada Buddhism has influenced and shaped the Lao character more than any other single force. *Theravada* means "Doctrine of the Elders." Its followers claim that it is a purer branch of Buddhism than the broader Mahayana, or "Great Vehicle," school. Theravada Buddhists believe their sect adheres more strictly to the teachings of the Buddha, as set down in the *Tripitaka* ("Three Baskets" in Sanskrit), the Buddhist scriptures. Theravada Buddhism, sometimes known as the "Little Vehicle," is practiced in Sri Lanka, Thailand, Burma, Cambodia, Sipsongpanna in China's Yunnan Province, and Laos.

Theravada Buddhism has influenced the Lao in their conduct and attitudes. Little emphasis is placed, for example, on the accumulation of wealth for its own gain. It is a common practice for the Lao to set aside a part of their slender funds as a donation for the upkeep of the local pagoda or monastery.

Traditionally, all Lao boys and men are expected to spend a period as a monk as a rite of passage—usually as a novice prior to marriage, but possibly in old age as well. Only a few women, usually elderly, become Buddhist nuns called *mae khao*; they also lead an ascetic life but, unlike monks, do not lead religious ceremonies.

ADVENT OF BUDDHISM

Fragments of Buddha statues dating back to the Khmer occupation of Laos in the eighth century have been found in the Vientiane area. Buddhism was practiced in this region as early as the second century. It was not until the arrival of Fa Ngum and the founding of the kingdom of Lan Xang, though, that Buddhism took root as an organized system of belief in Laos.

Fa Ngum was known in Laos as the Great Protector of the Faith. It was Fa Ngum who carried the Phra Bang, a small golden statue of the Buddha, from the Khmer court in Cambodia. The figure was originally cast in Sri Lanka before being taken to Angkor. It is of immense importance to the Lao, who regard it as the symbol of Lao Buddhism.

King Setthathirat championed the Buddhist faith in the sixteenth century by building many temples and monasteries. During Lan Xang's golden age, Vientiane became an important Buddhist center in Southeast Asia. Its importance was lost after many temples were destroyed by the Thai when they ravaged the city at the beginning of the nineteenth century.

Buddhism declined even further after 1975 under the Communist regime. People were prohibited from giving alms to monks, and the teaching of Buddhism was banned from primary schools. These days, with increasing government tolerance and support, however, Buddhism is undergoing a revival. With many being restored and redecorated, temples are lively centers of learning and worship again.

BUDDHIST TEACHINGS

Lao Buddhists try to follow the example of Siddhartha Gautama, the Buddha. Siddhartha's wanderings and meditations were rewarded when he attained enlightenment under a bodhi tree, after realizing the Four Noble Truths.

The Phra Bang Buddha, in the "Dispelling Fear" mudra, or position—with palms facing forward—is regarded as the most sacred and culturally significant image of the Buddha in Laos.

FOUR NOBLE TRUTHS The first Truth states that life consists of pain, suffering, disease, old age, and death. The second emphasizes that these are caused by desire and attachment to worldly things. The third Truth holds that detachment from such concerns can offer an end to suffering and the endless cycle of rebirth. The fourth Truth is that in order to free oneself from these, it is necessary to follow the Noble Eightfold Path.

THE EIGHTFOLD PATH This guide consists of right understanding, thought, speech, action, livelihood, effort, mindfulness, and concentration. This is known as the Middle Way. It avoids two extremes—the pursuit of happiness through pleasure, and self-inflicted pain.

THE FIVE PRECEPTS All good Buddhists try to follow the commands of the Buddha as expressed in the Five Precepts—do not take life, do not steal, do not commit adultery, do not speak falsely, and do not consume intoxicating drinks. Any diversion from these Five Precepts in daily life postpones the achievement of nirvana. The accumulation of merit, however, makes nirvana more attainable.

WHEEL OF REBIRTH The ultimate goal of all Buddhists is to free themselves from the tiresome cycle of existence and rebirth known as *samsara* so that they can enter *nirvana*. This ideal condition is often defined as "extinction of self" and can be described as a state of nothingness in which a Buddhist is finally free from suffering. In the Buddhist world view, the universe and all living forms are in a constant state of change from birth to death. After death comes the Wheel of Rebirth. There are three planes of existence in which beings can be reborn, depending on the thoughts, deeds, and speech of their previous life. These are the animal and ghost realms, the human plane, and the celestial one.

DHARMA The Buddha's teachings are known as the dharma. It is the responsibility of Buddhist monks to pass on these teachings to the people. The Buddhist clergy, or *sangha* (sang-GHER), the Buddha himself, and the dharma are known as the Triple Gem.

ALMSGIVING

There are various ways in which Lao Buddhists can gain merit. Good deeds, acts of generosity, and respect for elders are common means to gain merit in the next life. The pagoda, or *wat*, is the center of village life. Merit can be earned by donating money to the local Buddhist order, helping with the cost of building a new temple, sponsoring a religious ceremony, or paying for the ordination of a monk. Most young men will undergo a period of ordination at some stage in their lives. This is one effective way for a son to acquire merit for his family, especially because his mother and sisters, being women, cannot be ordained.

Monks depend upon the local population for most of their material needs. Pagodas are always located near population centers. Everyone has an opportunity to earn merit each morning by offering alms to monks as they walk through the streets at dawn asking for alms. In Laos it is mainly women who can be seen earning merit in this way. The women place rice, vegetables, and other delicacies into the monks' bowls as they pass.

Women give alms to Buddhist monks who collect the offerings daily in Luang Prabang.

IMAGES AND MUDRAS

Buddha images, especially statues, have survived war and destruction better than Lao temples. Unlike old bomb casings, bronze and gold Buddhas are never melted down, however ruinous their condition. Buddha images throng the insides of temples, monasteries, and sacred caves. They can be seen standing in the open along the roadside, commanding the crest of a hill, or ranged along the external pavilions of temples.

Apart from being works of art, they are also objects of worship. Images are represented in different *mudras*, or attitudes. Ancient Pali texts and Sanskrit poetry have set down certain characteristics of the Buddha that have influenced Lao artists.

The Buddha is usually represented sitting, standing, lying, or less commonly, walking. There are about forty mudras. Lao Buddhas have some unique features. These include elongated ears, a sharp beaked nose, and surprisingly slender waists. The following are some of the most popular mudras used in depicting the Buddha in Laos:

THE BUDDHA CALLING FOR RAIN In this mudra, the Buddha is standing with his hands pointing down toward the earth. This image is rarely found outside of Laos.

BHUMISPARCAMUDRA (boo-miss-PAH-cam-moo-DRAH) Also referred to as "Touching the Earth" or "Calling the Earth Goddess to Witness," this mudra depicts the Buddha's enlightenment and victory over Mara, king of the demons. The Buddha's right hand is placed over his right knee. His fingers point to the earth.

DHYANAMUDRA (yan-AH-moo-DRAH) This is a common image in which the Buddha is seen meditating. His open palms face upward, resting on his lap.

ABHAYAMUDRA (ab-hay-YAH-moo-DRAH) This means "Giving Protection" or "Dispelling Fear." The Buddha's right palm is usually raised in front of his chest as if holding back evil.

SPIRIT GROVES

Buddhism is the primary religion of the lowland Lao, but animism (spirit worship) is the dominant belief of many highland ethnic minorities such as the Hmong. They believe that spiritual beings inhabit certain forest groves. For most Lao, there is no contradiction in observing both Theravada Buddhism and animist practices. The Lao Loum's belief in *phi,* or spirits, plus the attendant superstitions and rituals coexist happily with Buddhism.

The belief in *phi* is often combined with ancestor worship. There are basically two types of spirits that the Lao pay attention to—mischievous or malignant ones and guardian spirits. Evil spirits may be spirits of the dead or spirits of a place. Lao villagers and mountain dwellers are careful to avoid jungles and lonely, unexplored places at night. One widespread belief is that it is dangerous to walk on all fours in the forest. Anyone who does this runs the risk of being possessed by a tiger spirit. It is also inadvisable to walk along a lonely riverbank at night in case a water spirit attacks. This would cause the person to believe he is a fish, and lengthy and costly offerings would have to be made to the spirit before the person could be released.

The Lao spend as much time making offerings to ensure the favor of the guardian spirits as they do to appease the evil ones. Rituals to Nang Prakosob, the female spirit of rice, for example, must be carefully observed to ensure a good harvest. Most villages have two main protective spirits—the *phi wat,* guardian of the temple, and the *phi muang*, protector of the village. In Vientiane the Chao Mae Si Muang is believed to be the guardian of the city. Local Lao go to Wat Si Muang to ask for her favor and make offerings.

OTHER RELIGIONS

Laos's 1991 constitution guarantees freedom of religious belief. The majority of Lao, however, feel comfortable and content with their unique mixture of Buddhism and animism and show little interest in converting to other faiths.

In the aftermath of the 1975 revolution, Christian missionaries were expelled from the country. The current Lao constitution forbids religious

Printing was only introduced to Laos in 1957. Before that, Lao literature was written in the manuscript form. Many manuscripts were engraved on palm leaves. Some of these have survived and are kept in museums or in the libraries of monasteries and temples.

Some of the most interesting manuscripts are those that contain the jataka *(jah-TAK-er) tales.*

The jataka *tales are central to Buddhist literature. This collection of stories concerns the previous* jataka, *incarnations or lives, of the Buddha. These former existences of the Buddha are called* Bodhisattvas.

The tales describe the long journey of the Buddha and his passage through the various animal states and human conditions to his final attainment of nirvana. The stories are a colorful vehicle for Hindu folklore and fables, the teaching of Buddhist ethics, satirical asides, and even humor. Fifty Lao jataka *recounting local folktales have been added to the original 547 tales that appear in Pali. The most popular* jataka *in Laos is the story of Prince Vessantara's perfect renunciation of the world, which is also known as* Phra Vet *in Lao.*

The stories are painted in bright colors on the outside walls of temples and shrines, often presented in panels that resemble a comic strip. The Lao enjoy the stories just as much for their entertainment value as for their religious and moral aspects.

proselytizing, or actively seeking to convert others to a particular religion. Foreigners caught distributing religious materials risk being arrested and deported.

Most Christians are found among either the French-educated Lao class that remained in the country after 1975 or the animist highland ethnic

THE PAK OU CAVES

The impressive Pak Ou Caves are located opposite the mouth of the Nam Ou River, a tributary of the Mekong, some 15 miles (24 km) north of Luang Prabang. They are set

dramatically into limestone cliffs overhanging the Mekong River. The upper cave is known as Tham Phun, the lower as Tham Thing. The two main caves are sanctuaries for thousands of Buddha images.

The caves were discovered by King Setthathirat in the sixteenth century. The statues, made of wood and gold, are more than three hundred years old. Many of them were brought here for safekeeping during periodic attacks on Luang Prabang. The statues vary in height from just a few inches to 6 feet (1.8 m). Many of the statues have been carved in classic attitudes such as the Buddha Calling for Rain.

Once inhabited by monks, the Loa people believe the caves are the home of guardian spirits. The Pak Ou Caves are sacred to the people, and a visit here is seen as a pilgrimage. Before the revolution, the Lao king used to visit the caves every year during the Pi Mai (Lao New Year) festival and conduct a candle-lighting ceremony. Hundreds of people still make the trip in boats from Luang Prabang during the festival to make offerings and light candles in the gloom of these sanctuaries.

minorities who were converted by Christian missionaries and priests operating under the umbrella of various nongovernmental organizations in the country's remote areas.

Islam has had little impact on Lao life—there are very few Muslims living in Vientiane. Most Lao Muslims are of Pakistani or Arab heritage. Many of them have married Lao women, who as spouses are given the constitutional right to convert to Islam. Others are descendants of the Cham Muslims from Cambodia, who fled Pol Pot's brutal persecution in the 1970s. A few groups of Muslim Yunnanese also live in northern Laos.

INTERNET LINKS

http://www.buddhanet.net/e-learning/buddhistworld/laos-txt.htm
Buddhism in Laos is covered on this site.

https://www.diamondway-buddhism.org/buddhism
This site explains Buddhism to Westerners.

http://factsanddetails.com/southeast-asia/Laos/sub5_3a/entry-2946.html
This site provides an overview of religion in Laos, with links to related topics.

https://www.state.gov/j/drl/rls/irf/2010/148878.htm
The US State Department reports on religious freedom in Laos.

https://www.theguardian.com/travel/gallery/2007/may/11/laos.culturaltrips
"The Life of a Lao Monk" is presented as a slideshow.

http://whc.unesco.org/en/list/479/video
This video about the life of Buddhist monks accompanies the World Heritage page for the town of Luang Prabang.

LANGUAGE

A Lao schoolgirl writes on a blackboard in her classroom.

9

LAO, SOMETIMES CALLED LAOTIAN, IS a language spoken by approximately 15 million people in Laos and northeast Thailand, where it is called the Isan language. The official language of the LPDR, Lao belongs to the Tai group of languages under the Tai-Kadai linguistic family. Tai is part of a language family that extends from Assam in India to Yunnan Province in southern China. There are Tai speakers in northern parts of Vietnam, Burma, Thailand, and pockets of China such as Guangxi and Sichuan. Together the number of speakers in the Tai language group is close to 900 million.

Standard Lao as spoken in the region around Vientiane has become the lingua franca of most Lao, including ethnic minorities who may have their own distinct languages and dialects. The Lao spoken today is quite different from the language spoken before the revolution. Many honorifics and other respectful forms of address disappeared as the regime tried to create a classless society. Large population movements after the war have introduced into the language local and regional words that have become part of a common, shared vocabulary.

Lao people have traditionally gone by only one name. They adopted surnames beginning in 1943 when the French colonial government mandated it, first of only royalty and the elite, but then across all classes. Wives usually take their husband's last name. Lao names are given in Western order, where the family name goes after the first given name. In remote areas, however, people today may still go by only one name.

THE TONAL SYSTEM

A stop sign in the Lao language.

Lao is a monosyllabic, tonal language. The verbs do not reflect tense. Most of the polysyllabic words found in Lao are borrowed from two ancient Indian languages, Pali and Sanskrit. Words have also crept in from Khmer, French, English, and even Persian. Spoken Lao uses six tones (variations of rising, high, mid, low, and falling). As with most other languages, the pitch at which the language is spoken is not absolute and will vary from speaker to speaker.

There are thirty-three consonants in Lao—twenty-seven are single consonants and six are double—which can be classified into three groups: low, high, and rising. Because almost all the high and rising consonants have identical sounds, the thirty-three consonants produce only twenty distinct sounds in all. There are twenty-eight vowel sounds in Lao. These are divided into long and short sounds. A slight change in inflection can drastically alter the meaning of a word. The word *khaa* (car), for example, can mean "crow" in a low level tone, "price" in the midtone, and "to kill" in a low, falling tone.

Although Lao grammar is surprisingly straightforward, the tonal system can, at least initially, be a stumbling block for foreigners wishing to learn the language.

THE LAO ALPHABET AND SCRIPT

Like Cambodian, Thai, and Burmese, written Lao has its origins in the ancient scripts of southern India. The oldest written documents still in existence in Laos date back to the sixteenth century.

Lao manuscripts, or *kampi* (kem-PI), were usually engraved on palm leaves and then threaded together with cord. Sets of twenty leaves were bundled together and wrapped in cloth for safekeeping, but many have suffered from the passage of time, the tropical climate, and insect attacks.

Other scripts have been used throughout the centuries in Laos. These include scripts for spoken Yao and for written Pali, a Thai Neua tribal script, and a Chinese-based system used in the sixteenth century.

Modern Lao is written from left to right. There are no spaces between words; rather, spaces in a Lao text indicate the end of a clause or sentence. The alphabet has no upper or lower case differentiation. The letters are consonants, while the vowels are indicated with symbols or diacritic marks above, below, or around the consonant. The letters do not correspond to the Roman alphabet in any way. The letters and numerals are curved and looping, with no sharp corners or crosses.

There were four spelling systems in use before the revolution. These have been standardized into one single phonetic script that expresses both the sound of the word and its pitch.

Handwritten labels describe the contents of bags of goods for sale at a street market in Vientiane.

ROMANIZATION

Romanization, in linguistics, is the transcription into the Latin alphabet (used in English and other Western languages) of a language based on a different writing system. Romanizing helps nonnative speakers try to approximate

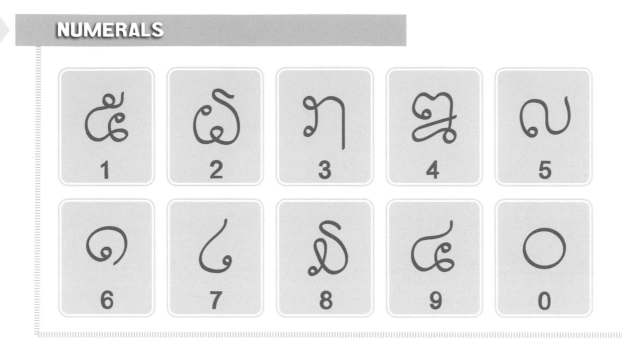

the sounds of the language. Romanizing tonal languages like Lao is different because the Latin alphabet provides no tonal guidance in itself. Other transcription problems arise for sounds that have no equivalent in the respective languages.

For Lao, there is no official Romanization format specifically for Lao. There are, however, several different universal transcription systems, including the IPA (International Phonetic Alphabet) and ALA-LC romanization standard of the American Library Association—Library of Congress.

LAO AND THAI

The Lao and the Thai understand each other reasonably well. Standard Thai is similar enough to Lao for the two to be mutually intelligible, much like the relationship between spoken Portuguese and Spanish. Most of the present-day differences stem from the French colonial period, when Lao was insulated from ongoing changes in the Thai language.

A Thai dialect spoken in the north of Thailand, particularly its northeastern province of Esan—which was originally part of the Lao kingdom of Lan Xang—

is virtually the same as Lao. Curiously, there are supposedly more Lao speakers living in this region of Thailand than there are in Laos itself.

Because most of the textbooks used at the university level were and continue to some extent to be in Thai, many educated Lao can understand the written script as well. Thanks to the popularity of Thai television and radio programs that are transmitted daily over the Mekong, almost all Lao can understand spoken Thai.

A sign for an emergency room is written in Thai, Lao, and English.

LANGUAGES OF THE MINORITIES

Russian linguists in the 1980s estimated that the highland ethnic minorities of Laos had more than six hundred spoken dialects. Numerous local dialects, branches, and subdivisions of Tai languages are mutually intelligible to the respective groups. With the exception of one or two groups such as the Yao, very few of the tribal groups have their own written script. Important language families that exist among the highland ethnic peoples of Laos include:

TIBETO-BURMESE The Lahu, the Lisu, and the Akha are examples of tribes that speak dialects within this group. They are mostly concentrated in the northern region of Laos.

HMONG-YAO This important group originated in southern China and includes the Munlanguage of the Lanten. Groups of Hmong are found in China, Thailand, and northern Vietnam.

MON-KHMER More than thirty tribal groups speak dialects that fall into this language family. The best known are the Alak, the Soh, and the Suei, who live in the south; the Lamet, from the north; and the Pai and the Khamu, who can be found all over Laos.

ທ່ານຮູ້ບໍ່ວ່າ?

DID YOU KNOW?

TAT KUANG SI RESCUE CENTRE

ມີໝີສອງຊະນິດຢູ່ ສ ປ ປ ລາວ
ໝີດຳ ແລະ ເໝີຍ. ໝີໝາ(ເໝີຍ)
ແມ່ນນ້ອຍກວ່າ
ໝີດຳ ແລະມັນມີຂົນສິນຳຕານສັ້ນ
ແລະຢູ່ຄຳຈະ ເປັນແຖບສິເຫຼືອງກວ່າໝີດຳ.

There are two species of bear found in Laos: The Asiatic Black bear and the Malayan Sun bear.

Sun bears are smaller than moon bears and have shorter dark brown fur with a rounder, more yellow chest marking.

Information on a sign at the Kuang Si bear rescue center near Luang Prabang is provided in English primarily for tourists.

FRENCH AND ENGLISH

Up until the early 1990s, French was the preferred second language of the educated Lao class, government workers, and administrators. Even now it remains the country's unofficial second language. Shop signs, restaurant menus, and some legal documents are often still written in French with Lao translations. The language is falling out of favor among the younger generation, however, who associate it with colonialism.

Like their neighbors in Vietnam and Cambodia, young Lao prefer to learn English instead of French. They believe that a basic knowledge of English will enhance their career prospects, especially in the fledgling tourism sector, and help them acquire high-paying jobs.

PROVERBIALLY YOURS

Lao, in common with other languages, contains a rich and colorful assortment of proverbs. Many reflect aspects of the national character and ways of thinking, the nation's culture, the folklore of the highland ethnic peoples, and even the geographical features of the country. The following is a small selection from the hundreds that exist in the Lao language:

When one has heard, one must listen, and when one has seen, one must judge with one's heart.

Medicine can cure the bite of a poisonous snake, but nothing can master a wicked heart.

When the buffaloes fight, it is the grass that suffers.

A tray full of money is not worth a mind full of knowledge.

Some are brave in the village but cowards in the forest.

When the water level falls, the ants eat the fish. When the level rises, the fish eat the ants.

An empty pot makes a loud noise.

Do not soil the shade of a tree that has been hospitable to you.

INTERNET LINKS

http://factsanddetails.com/southeast-asia/Laos/sub5_3b/entry-2945.html
This page provides a good overview of Lao language and related topics.

https://www.omniglot.com/writing/lao.htm
Omniglot provides a good basic introduction to Lao.

ARTS

Colorful embroidery decorates a piece of Lao silk.

LITERATURE

Lao literature, like that of neighboring Thailand and Cambodia, presents a strong imprint of Indian influence. Laos has a strong oral tradition—folk stories were recited, while epic poems and verse novels were usually sung or chanted by professional storytellers and balladeers. The most famous work in Lao literature, an epic poem called *Sin Xay,* was originally sung.

The arrival of Buddhism in the fourteenth century introduced more Lao to the written language. People began recording the stories they had heard. Classical tales focus on love, heroic deeds, mythology, and the history of the gods. Religious literature, such as the *jataka* tales, deals with the Buddha's birth and various forms of existence. One popular story involves a legend about the Buddha footprint found on Mount Phousi in Luang Prabang. Unfortunately many Lao manuscripts were taken to Bangkok after the Thai razed the capital in 1828.

Historical chronicles were traditionally written in Pali by anonymous authors. The best known is *Nithan Khun Borom* (*The History of King Khun Borom*). Many Lao popular stories and novels are based on the Indian canon of tales called *Panchatantra,* where adventurous and supernatural themes dominate. Tales about animals who have human characteristics are also popular. Some are reminiscent of Aesop's fables. These are contained in several volumes of stories titled *The Bull*, *The Frogs*, *The Demons*, and *The Birds*. Echoes of another familiar story, *Cinderella*, can be found in the Lao tale *Pa Pul Dan*, about a young girl and her selfish stepmother.

Laos has a short history of written literature. Printing was introduced during French colonial rule, and the country's first modern novel, *The Sacred Buddha Image*, was published in 1944. Decades of civil war followed by Communist rule have hampered literary development, as the population

The abbot of a Buddhist temple in the village of Muang Vaen explains some illustrated manuscripts telling the story of Sin Xay.

NAGA SYMBOLISM

Lao art and legends are full of stories and images of naga *(NAR-ger). The* naga, *or phaya* nak *(nak), as it is better known in Laos, is a mythical water serpent that resembles a cobra. It was an important symbol in Southeast Asia even before the advent of Buddhism or Hinduism in the region.*

The naga is a symbol of both destruction and renewal. In Hindu-Buddhist legends, a naga was responsible for causing a great drought to spread over the earth after it drank all the water. An ancient Khmer legend relates how a king, whose domains were suffering from a terrible drought, fired rockets into the sky; the god Shiva was so pleased that he let the rains fall. Many of the rockets used in the May Rocket Festival are decorated to resemble nagas.

Buddha is believed to have been protected by the hood of a naga when facing the demon Mara. Naga images appear all over Laos. Their mouths are always open, and their heads may look like those of snakes or dragons. Naga heads frequently support the roofs of temples. Temple entrances are often guarded by five- or seven-headed nagas. Single nagas, their bodies stretched to fantastic lengths, may decorate the balustrades of staircases leading up to hilltop temples. They are placed there to symbolize a bridge between two worlds—the earthly and the spiritual. They provide a good example of the way ancient myths, legends, and folk symbolism in Laos are interwoven with orthodox Buddhism.

has been more concerned with day-to-day living than with the arts. Popular author Ounthine Bounyavong's *Mother's Beloved: Stories from Laos* was published in 1999. It was the first instance of contemporary Lao fiction.

TEMPLE ARCHITECTURE

Architecturally, the most important buildings in Laos are *wats* (Buddhist temples, sometimes spelled "*vats*") and *thats* (Buddhist stupas, or shrines, built to hold religious objects). Wats are characterized by steep tiled roofs, with frescoes and mosaic decorations on the walls depicting the events of Buddha's life. Lao-style thats have a distinctive curvilinear, four-cornered shape, representing the unfurling of a lotus flower.

WAT XIENG THONG Wat Xieng Thong is the most important royal temple in Luang Prabang. Built in 1559 by King Setthathirat, it is the only building of

A glass mosaic "tree of life" decorates an exterior wall of the Wat Xieng Thong.

The combination of high ground and water guaranteed that Phu Pasak, near Champasak in southern Laos, would be a sacred place. The priests of Chenla, the civilization that preceded the Khmer, erected shrines to the mountain gods and water spirits here. A temple already stood at this spot as early as the sixth century.

Vat Phou (also spelled Wat Phou), the country's great Khmer temple, was built in the tenth century as a shrine to the Hindu deity Shiva. Archaeologists believe that there may have been a road directly connecting Vat Phou with Angkor, 60 miles (97 km) away in Cambodia.

Well-preserved reliefs of Hindu gods and goddesses still decorate the temple's ruined facades. Vat Phou was later converted into a Buddhist temple. The mountain and its sacred spring behind the temple have been the sites of worship and meditation for religious hermits since the eleventh century.

The temple complex is a UNESCO World Heritage Site.

Boun Vat Phou, a three-day Buddhist festival, is held at the temple on the full moon of the third lunar month. The festival, which has its origins in the spirit cults of the south, was originally held to appease the guardian phi of Vat Phou, and human sacrifices were conducted. Today they have been replaced with a buffalo sacrifice. The festival is one of the largest in Laos. Pilgrims arrive from the south of Laos as well as from neighboring Thai districts. The water tanks at Vat Phou are used for boat racing. Music and dance performances, fireworks, elephant races, and buffalo fights add to the festivities. Buddhism as well as animist rituals incorporating elements of Hinduism are practiced side by side.

Golden wood carvings adorn the wat's interior.

its kind to have survived the succession of raids that plagued the city in the nineteenth century.

Xieng Thong means "the golden city." It also means "flame tree." The rear temple wall contains a glass mosaic representation of the *thong* (thong), or tree of life. Mosaic decoration is a relatively recent art form. Colored mosaics depicting local village and court life cover the compounds of two *hor song phra* (hor-son-PHRA), or red side chapels, in Wat Xieng Thong.

Considered by many to be the most beautiful *wat* in Laos, Wat Xieng Thong embodies all the elegance and refinement of Lao religious architecture. Its breathtakingly dramatic roof is in the Luang Prabang style. Layers overlap one another in a complex and graceful design that swoops so low, they appear to almost touch the ground. Ornate, gold-stenciled designs cover the exterior walls, while the interior contains gold and bronze Buddhas, embroidered tapestries, and finely carved wooden columns.

The Wat Mai
Monastery
is another
architectural
masterpiece in
Luang Prabang.

WAT MAI The name Wat Mai means "the new monastery," and it's another Lao architectural treasure. The temple, which is topped with a distinctive five-tiered red roof, took more than seventy years to complete. The veranda ceiling, which displays lotus blossoms and scenes from the Buddha's life, is one of the best-preserved murals of its kind in Laos.

Wat Mai's most striking feature is the extraordinary golden bas-relief that runs along the facade. This tells the story of the Phravet, one of the last incarnations of the Buddha. Set in a rural background, it depicts scenes of village life that are clearly Lao. A closer look even reveals small depictions of Luang Prabang landmarks such as That Chomsi and Wat Xieng Thong. The episodes read like a text from left to right. A long beam above the frieze, carved in red and gold relief, highlights settings from the Ramayana.

WOOD CARVING

The Lao have long excelled at wood carving and engraving. Sophisticated craftsmen have been producing decorative religious art for centuries. Large scrolled teak panels on the sides of temples relate scenes from the Ramayana or local myths.

The wooden doors and window shutters of temples are usually decorated with elaborate foliage and figures that fill the surface in tight but harmonious patterns. These are often painted red and gilded. The gables of temple roofs are made of richly decorated, carved panels in wood and stucco. The roof edges curve upward in order to catch evil spirits.

Many distinctive Buddha statues are made of wood, and fine examples can be seen in the many temples dotting Vientiane and Luang Prabang. An ornate royal funerary chariot at Wat Xieng Thong is made from carved and gilded wood. The chariot's prow is shaped into the form of a five-headed *naga*.

High quality wood carvings and sculptures are also found on the doors, shutters, and gables of recently renovated or reconstructed temples, proving that the art is still very much alive in Laos.

Carved warriors tell a story in wood on the walls of the Wat Xieng Thong temple.

LAOTIAN LOOMS

Traditionally Lao women have expressed themselves creatively by weaving highly complex textiles.

Lao weavers are among the finest in Southeast Asia. Textiles are very important to all Tai societies. In Laos the continued popularity of the women's national dress has helped to sustain an art that has vanished elsewhere.

In traditional Lao society, an ability to weave was a prerequisite for marriage. Even today, especially among the highland ethnic minorities, it is believed that the best way to a man's heart is through a woman's weaving. A woman who is known to be a deft weaver accrues more status than an average weaver.

Looms are often located among the piles that support the house, as this is a cool and shady place to work. Cotton and silk are spun by hand. There is only one cotton harvest a year, but silk can be harvested four times annually. Silk weavers must feed the worms with mulberry leaves to get good yields.

The French introduced chemical dyes to Laos. Since the revolution, there has been a revival in the use of dyes from natural sources. These take longer to obtain. To expert eyes, however, these colors are much richer and more saturated. Red comes from breadfruit and rain trees, indigo from the indigo plant, black from pounded ebony seeds, and yellow from turmeric roots.

Buddhist and animist symbols often appear as traditional motifs in Lao textiles. Other common themes include flowers, hooks, diamonds, nagas, casuarina trees, and stylized figures of peacocks, elephants, geese, and dragons. Many old techniques and designs have been lost because of war and population displacement among ethnic groups that were leading exponents of the weaving traditions. It is vital that these old skills be renewed as soon as possible, before they are lost forever.

INTERNET LINKS

http://factsanddetails.com/southeast-asia/Laos/sub5_3c/entry-2966.html
This site has a great deal of information about Lao arts and culture, but no pictures.

http://www.newworldencyclopedia.org/entry/Laotian_art
A good overview of traditional and contemporary arts in Laos is provided on this site.

http://www.nytimes.com/2007/09/23/travel/tmagazine/10get-sourcing-txt.html?mcubz=0
The New York Times presents a travel article about weaving in Laos.

http://www.plainofjars.net//dance.htm
This site offers some audio clips of Lao music, traditional and contemporary.

https://theartofhmongembroidery.wordpress.com/tag/traditional-hmong-clothes
Many examples of Hmong embroidered clothing are pictured on this site.

http://whc.unesco.org/en/list/481
The official World Heritage listing for Vat Phou includes a number of slides.

LEISURE

A woman talks to her granddaughter on a laptop by way of Skype.

11

Only about 18 percent of the Lao people have regular access to the Internet.

YEARS OF WAR AND DEPRIVATION have obliged the population to maintain a traditional way of life that continues relatively unchanged, especially in rural areas. Leisure activities revolve, as they always have, around the pleasures of family life, the community, and religious practices.

The pursuit of leisure, in the Western sense of the word, is a concept that applies only to the wealthy or more fashion-conscious in Lao cities. Few people are familiar with sports and pastimes such as tennis and golf. Computer and video games are virtually unheard of.

For most Lao, the notion of developing a hobby or setting aside time for planned leisure activities is unusual. The Lao are noted for being a relaxed and easygoing people. They believe that an activity is best avoided if it is not fun, because it will probably cause stress. Lao do not have to be told to slow down and relax. The attitude is inbred.

Festivals are important to the Lao, as they provide the chance for family gatherings. Highland ethnic groups often visit Lao cities to participate in festivities or to sell their wares to the lowland Lao. There is rarely spare money for holidays or excursions. Pleasure is derived from the simple, enduring things in life.

Many Lao enjoy tuning into entertainment programs from neighboring countries. They have six television broadcast stations, three government operated and three commercial. Nearly all programming is relayed by way of satellite. Only about 1,266,000 homes have telephones.

HERBAL SAUNAS

The residents of Vientiane have long been able to enjoy healthy relaxation in the form of traditional saunas. These are found in some of the city's temples. The best-known temple for this kind of treatment is Wat Sok Pa Luang, a retreat on the outskirts of Vientiane. The saunas are prepared by Buddhist nuns.

Herbs are mixed with dried eucalyptus and other leaves and burned underneath an elevated wooden sauna room in which four or five people can sit. The pleasant fragrance of burning sap and herbs can be inhaled. The saunas are usually conducted in the early evening. Herbal teas are served on an airy balcony between sessions in the sauna.

The Lao say that for maximum effect, it is best to allow the herbs to soak into the pores of the skin for at least two hours before one takes a bath.

CITY PASTIMES

Fast-modernizing Vientiane provides city dwellers with a diverse range of leisure activities. Popular pastimes include window shopping in the capital's stores and hanging out at cafés with friends.

Film is a universal pleasure, and going to the movies is a popular pastime with the Lao. The country has no film industry of its own, so most films are dubbed into Lao from Tamil and Mandarin. Thai films are usually shown in their original versions. Very few Lao dine at restaurants, but those who can afford it socialize at bars and beer gardens dotting the banks of rivers. For the people of Vientiane a trip out to one of the cafés, bars, or stalls that have sprung up around the Friendship Bridge has become a popular excursion. Young people are more inclined, though, to spend their time motorbiking around town; listening to mainstream Lao pop, which resembles Thai-style music; or attending one of Vientiane's nightly discos.

Children choose music and movie CDs on sale in a village shop on the southwestern Nakai Plateau.

Young men play takraw in Luang Namtha Province.

SPORTS AND GAMES

Part of the Communist ideology of the post-1975 era was to develop a healthy and vigorous nation through sports. Most Lao cities have a sports stadium. Some were built at the expense of other civil amenities such as good roads. Sports stadiums also serve as venues for concerts, National Day celebrations, and political rallies. In cities such as Vientiane, soccer teams regularly work out in the stadiums, and many Lao are immensely proud of their national team.

Another popular pastime is *takraw* (TAHK-raw), a traditional game played with a hollow cane ball. Two teams compete across a net. The players must keep the ball in the air for as long as possible using only their feet, heels, shoulders, and elbows. A skillful team may be able to keep several balls in the air at the same time. *Takraw* is also widely played in Thailand, Burma, and Malaysia. In former times, the game received royal patronage. These days it is undergoing a popular revival.

Lao-style boxing is a form of martial art called Muay Lao (MAE-Lao). It was banned under the French but is now enjoying a revival thanks to the efforts of the government-sponsored Lao Sports Association. The carved pillars and stone slabs of ancient Lao temples often depict a variety of poses and steps that are part of the training. The troops of Fa Ngum, the king who first unified the country, are said to have found the discipline useful in battle. Both feet and fists are used in this sport, which resembles a fusion of boxing and karate.

A young athlete practices his moves at a Muay Lao tournament in a rural village near Vientiane.

INTERNET LINKS

http://www.goabroad.net/Brooklynmonk/journals/1197/Muay-Lao,-the-forgotten-art-of-kickboxing
This article is a first-hand report on the sport of Muay Lao.

https://www.thewholeworldornothing.com/blog/wat-sok-pa-luang-monks-massage-and-meditation-in-vientiane/2016/11
Some Westerners travel to Wat Sok Pa Luang and report on their experience there.

http://www.topendsports.com/world/countries/laos.htm
This is a quick look at sports in Laos.

FESTIVALS

Lao girls prepare to cheer the home team at the Southeast Asian Games at the national stadium in Vientiane.

12

LAO FESTIVALS HAVE MUCH IN common with those in other Southeast Asian countries, particularly Thailand. What makes Lao festivals unique is their retention of many original elements that have been lost or rejected elsewhere. Less commercialized than neighboring countries' cultural events and more elemental and closer to their animist roots, Lao festivals represent the closest link to many of the pre-Buddhist rites and practices that once thrived throughout the region.

The Lao are a festive people, a fact attested to by the number and wealth of national and local festivals held throughout the year. *Boun* (boon) means "festival" in Lao. *Het boun* (HET-boon) signifies "merit making," so *boun*, to the Lao way of thinking, is an opportunity for self-improvement through religious observance and the pursuit of earthly pleasures.

In Laos, the color white is a symbol of peace, harmony, good fortune, and human warmth and community. The cotton threads used in the *baci* ceremony are always white.

Hmong teens throw balls in a traditional game as they celebrate the new year.

The Lao are happy to celebrate not only their own festivals but those of other groups and cultures as well. New Year's Day is celebrated four times a year: the international New Year in January; the Chinese and Vietnamese New Year (also known as Tet) in January/February; the Lao Buddhist New Year, which falls in April; and finally the Hmong New Year in December.

THE LAO CALENDAR

The Western Gregorian calendar is used in Laos for all government and business matters. Many people, however, especially in rural areas, still refer to the traditional lunar calendar. The Lao Buddhist calendar is based on the movements of the sun and the moon. Each year is reckoned to begin in December, but the Lao choose to celebrate the beginning of the year in April, which is considered a more auspicious month.

The Lao calendar is a combination of the old Khmer and Sino-Vietnamese ones, in which each year is named after a different animal. During the Lao New Year celebrations, paper pennants bearing images of the animal for that year are sold. Because the Lao Buddhist year follows a lunar calendar, the timing of many festivals varies from year to year.

The Festive Year Includes The Following Holidays And Observances.

January
Boun Pha Vet . . . . *Celebrates Prince Vessantara's Reincarnation As Buddha.*

Late January/February
Chinese New Year And Vietnamese Tet . . . *A Time For Lion Dances, Processions, And Fireworks.*

February
Magha Puja . . . . . . *Celebrated On The Full Moon Of The Third Lunar Month; Commemorates Buddha Preaching To The Spontaneous Arrival Of 1,250 Monks.*

April
Lao New Year (Boun Pi Mai). . . . . *Year's Biggest Holiday Is Also A Water Festival.*

May
Labor Day . . . . *May 1 Honors Workers With Parades And A Day Off From Work.*
Visakha Puja . . . . *A Festival Celebrating The Birth, Enlightenment, And Death Of The Buddha.*

May/June
The Rocket Festival (Boun Bang Fay). . . *A Buddhist Rain-Making Festival For The Planting Season.*

July
Khao Phansa . . . . *The Beginning Of The Three Month-Long Buddhist Fast. All Monks Stay Inside Their Temple For Prayer And Meditation. A Time For Religious Retreats And Fasting.*

August/September
Haw Khao Padap Din . . . . . *The Living Pay Respects To The Dead. Buried Bodies Are Exhumed And Cleaned. Many Cremations Are Held At This Time.*

October
Awk Phansa . . . . . . *Full Moon Marks The End Of The Three-Month Buddhist Fast. Parties Are Held, And Boat Races Take Place On The Mekong River.*
Bun Nam . . . . *Water Festival Celebrates Awk Phansa With Boat Races And Lai Hua Fai (Fireboat) Festival.*

November
That Luang . . . . *A Colorful Event Held At The Country's Most Important Temple.*

December
Lao National Day . . . . *Celebrates The 1975 Revolution With Flags, Parades And Speeches.*

MAJOR FESTIVALS

While there are many small annual *boun* celebrated at local pagodas, there are also several major regional celebrations, such as the Wat Phu Festival in Champasak in the south. The four most important festivals in Laos are the Lao New Year (Pi Mai), the Rocket Festival (Boun Bang Fay), the Water Festival (Boun Lay Heua Fay), and the That Luang Festival (Boun That Luang).

PI MAI

Few festivals evoke the life and customs of the people better than the Lao New Year, or Pi Mai. Pi Mai is known in Laos as the Fifth Month Festival.

Lao astrologers decided to delay the official year by several months so that the New Year would start under more favorable conditions. The astrological signs at this particular time are believed to point to light and prosperity. The period also anticipates the end of the hot season and the advent of the life-sustaining rains.

Local folks throw water to celebrate the new year at a water festival in April.

Before the festival begins, each house is meticulously cleaned and swept to banish evil spirits. Temples and homes also receive a fresh coat of paint.

The festival is an occasion for the Lao to dress up in their best and visit temples. The Lao pray for a good crop and pay homage to the city's most important Buddha statues. It is the monks' task to ritually cleanse Buddha images with perfumed holy water filled with flowers. Water is a strong symbol of purification. Often monks and passersby on the streets are doused with pails of water.

Khmu villagers perform a Baci ceremony for visitors.

Votive mounds in the shape of miniature stupas are constructed with sand in the compounds of temples or along the banks of the Mekong River. Pi Mai is a serious occasion but not a solemn one. During the day and evening Vientiane is alive with parades, beauty contests, musical and dance recitals, dramas, and fairs.

The Lao are staunchly conservative and traditional people. During Pi Mai, young Lao visit their families, elders, and superiors to pay their respect. Kneeling humbly before their elders, they pour fragrant water over their hands and seek blessings and good fortune for the coming year.

BACI CEREMONY

The *baci* ceremony is unique to Tai peoples and central to Lao culture. The animist ritual is believed to predate Buddhism. Baci are held to celebrate special events and occasions such as marriages, births, visits from guests, and homecomings.

They are also held during festivals and private parties. In Laos novice monks are given a baci before they enter the wat, mothers are honored with one after they have recovered from giving birth, and visiting officials often receive a baci. Baci are usually conducted by a respected elder, sometimes in the presence of a monk.

Besides generating goodwill and hospitality, the baci aims to restore balance and harmony to the individual and the community. The ceremony is also dedicated to the sick in the hope of providing a cure. The Lao believe that the body is protected by thirty-two spirits or vital life forces called *kwan* (KWA-ang). For a person to enjoy perfect health and balance, all thirty-two kwan must be present. The departure of even one will bring about illness and even possible death. As guests pray on, the person conducting the ritual chants in a mix of Lao and Pali, invoking both Buddhist and animist deities and spirits, all the while calling for the kwan to return.

Central to the ceremony is an arrangement of flowers, white cotton strings, banana leaves, and candles called a *pha kwan* (PA-kwang). White threads are taken from the pha kwan and tied around the guests' wrists with blessings and good wishes. The threads should not be removed for at least three days. A meal is served after the ceremony. This is often followed by the *lam vong*, the national dance.

This ancient ceremony is deeply important as a social, family, and spiritual event which confirms the value of life.

THE ROCKET FESTIVAL

Like the *baci* ceremony, Boun Bang Fay, or the Rocket Festival, is a good example of the Lao propensity to mix Buddhism and animism. *Bang* (BA-an) means "bamboo pipe," and *fay* (fey) is "fire." The festival is traditionally held on the day of the full moon during the sixth month of the lunar calendar.

The official purpose of the festival is to commemorate the life and achievements of the Buddha. Pilgrimages and merit making are important parts of the events. A more earthy side to the festival, harking back to ancient fertility rites, is associated with the rockets themselves. These are fired into the sky in the symbolic hope of releasing the rains.

The rockets, which are covered in aluminium foil and colorful streamers, are made of bamboo and may be as long as 6 feet (1.8 m). The rockets are carried through the streets to the accompaniment of drums, *khene*, and songs. The rocket that soars the highest will bring the most prestige to its makers.

In former times, the rockets were made exclusively by the temple authorities. Today they are made by villages, government departments, schools, and trade union groups as well.

For visitors, the festival is a good chance to enjoy Lao music and dance, as well as performances of *maw Loum* (moor LOOM), a traditional folk musical that is both bawdy and comical. For rural Lao, Boun Bang Fay is the last chance for high spirits before the hard work in the rice fields begins in earnest.

A homemade rocket soars to the sky during the annual Rocket Festival in May 2016.

INTERNET LINKS

http://www.laoheritagefoundation.org/ceremonies/baci.jsp
This site describes the baci ceremony and its various elements and symbols.

http://www.laos-guide-999.com/Lao-festivals.html
This guide covers the majors holidays in Laos with links to related articles.

https://www.timeanddate.com/holidays/laos
This site provides the current calendar of events in Laos.

FOOD

Colorful fruits and vegetables are for sale at the morning market in Luang Prabang.

13

LAO CUISINE IS BASED ON RICE. Glutinous, or sticky, rice is the main staple, and dishes are liberally doused with spices such as ginger, tamarind, lemongrass, and several types of hot chili peppers. A typical Lao dish is a mixture of fiery and fragrant flavors, moderated by herbs. Because the country has no access to the sea, fish come fresh from the Mekong and other rivers.

Padek (pah DEK), or fermented fish, and *nam pla* (nahm PLAH), or fish sauce, are vital staples—though their distinctive smells take some getting used to. Food is usually prepared on a stove fired by wood or charcoal.

The kitchen garden commands an important place in Lao homes. Vegetables such as onions, yams, cucumbers, salad greens, eggplants, beans, spinach, and shallots are grown there. Condiments such as citronella, hot peppers, and ginger may also be cultivated. Each house normally has its own fruit trees as well. Residents simply reach out and pluck bananas, coconuts, mangoes, avocados, lychees, guavas, and durians from their gardens when the fruit are in season. These home products supplement food that is bought in the open market.

The Lao eat with a fork in the left hand and a spoon in the right. The fork is used to push food onto the spoon. Sticky rice, however, is eaten with the fingers of the right hand, which are cleaned with a napkin. The rice is often formed into a ball and dipped into the dishes and used for mopping up like bread. Laotians generally don't use chopsticks, except for eating noodles and noodle soups.

Smiling boys
eat rice with
their hands.

BASKETS OF RICE

Rice is highly esteemed in Laos. The Lao are especially partial to sticky or glutinous rice, *khao niao* (kah-OH nya-o). Family members may eat from a communal bowl or have their own individual baskets. Sticky rice is eaten with the fingers. Rice is rolled into a tight ball and then used as an eating utensil to push and scoop up other ingredients on the plate or is dipped into sauces.

The sweet-toothed Lao also add rice to various desserts and sweets. The versatile grain can be mixed with taro, coconut milk, or water-lily roots. *Khao tom* (kah-OH tom) consists of rice combined with coconut milk and bananas and then steamed in a banana leaf. Another popular dessert, *tom nam hua bua* (tom nahm WHOO-er boo-er), is prepared by mixing coconut milk and lotus flowers.

Rice remains a powerful, life-affirming symbol throughout Asia. In Laos sticky rice is often pressed onto Buddha statues and the walls of private homes as offerings to the resident spirit. Women are strongly associated with rice. In many remote villages, a legend holds that the rice goddess sacrificed her body in a fire, and the ashes helped to produce a bumper crop for the village. In some Phuan villages, the bones of female ancestors are preserved in a stupa in the middle of the family's rice fields.

POPULAR DISHES

In addition to freshwater fish, the Lao get their protein from pork, chicken, water buffalo, and duck. Deer, quail, wild chickens, and small birds are also eaten. The traditional ceremonial dish of the Lao and the closest thing to a national dish is called *laap* (laap) or *larb*. (Other spellings include *laab*, *lahb*, and *larp*.) The word means "luck." Laap is an indispensable dish for special occasions and for honored guests. Often compared with steak tartar or Mexican seviche, meat-based laap is made by mixing finely minced beef, chicken, pork, and venison. The dish can be made with finely minced raw or cooked meats or fish, usually mixed with roasted ground rice, chilis, mint, and other herbs, sliced onions or scallions, fish sauce (nam pla), and lime juice.

A wealth of traditional street food offerings are on display at a stall in Luang Prabang.

A man sells French-style baguette sandwiches at a street market in Vientiane.

It is served at room temperature accompanied by sticky rice and raw vegetables.

Spicy green papaya salad, *tam maak hoong* (taam MAK hoong), is another favorite. This is made by pounding unripe, green papaya, lime juice, chilies, garlic, and padek (fermented fish sauce) in a big mortar.

Thai-style curries are popular as well. These dishes are spiced with numbingly hot red chilies but cooled down with the use of slightly sweet coconut milk. The Lao also enjoy Vietnamese food. The most common dish is *pho* (fuh)—a rice-noodle soup. Pho is usually served with a side plate of salad vegetables such as lettuce, mint, and bean sprouts, which can be added to the broth. Pho is a popular snack and breakfast dish. Soup accompanies most main meals and is always served in the middle or toward the end, never at the beginning.

FRENCH LEGACIES

Many of the old French buildings in Laos may be crumbling, but the French food legacy is as strong as ever. French cuisine is widely available in Vientiane and Luang Prabang. Frog legs and filet mignon, a steak dish, remain popular with Lao who can afford such luxuries. French-style baguettes are common breakfast items. These are sold fresh at the morning markets and bakeries. The bread is dipped into hot milky coffee and eaten with fried eggs or condensed milk. Alternatively one can tuck into baguettes the Lao way: sprinkle fish sauce on top or make a sandwich with a pâté filling.

French croissants and *pains au chocolat* (pan o sho-co-LA), or rolls filled with chocolate, are eaten in street cafés with cups of strong Lao coffee. Visitors to Vientiane are often surprised to find bottles of old wines such

as Bordeaux and Bergerac being proudly carried from the cellars of French restaurants.

A family in the remote Sainyabuli Province sits cross-legged around their dinner.

MANNERS AT A LAO TABLE

Lao family meals seem like relaxed and informal events, but there are certain customs and manners to be observed. Unlike in Western countries, where people sit around a raised table, the Lao are more likely to squat on the floor around one or more circular bamboo tables. Instead of a succession of courses served one after the other, food is laid out on the table in several dishes at the beginning of the meal. The family and any guests help themselves, eating whatever they like in no particular order.

There are certain attitudes connected to food and its consumption that foreigners may not be aware of. One of these is the Lao concept of *piep* (pyee-EP). It can be roughly translated as "status," "dignity," or "sense of prestige." At Lao family meals, this means that elders and the most senior-ranking members of the family always take the first mouthful. Other members follow according to age. From this point onward everyone is free to eat whatever they fancy, but no one should help himself before an older family member has first tried a dish. It is also inadvisable to reach for food at the same time as someone else. Guests should not continue eating after everyone else has finished. It is the custom in Laos to always leave something on the plate when one has finished the meal. If a guest does not do this, the host will lose piep, as it is understood that he did not provide enough food, leaving the guest hungry.

The Lao are meticulously clean and have the habit of washing their hands not only before but also after a meal.

DRINKS

The Lao enjoy natural drinks such as coconut milk and their own local brew *lau-lao* (LA-oo-lao), which is a fermented rice wine. Coconut milk is often

A fruit shake stand offers fresh smoothie-style drinks.

mixed with other fruit juices, while white lau-lao is sometimes enjoyed with a twist of lime or even with cola. *Fan thong* (fahn-TONG) is a red lau-lao fermented with herbs. It is the custom at parties, festivals, and other social gatherings for several people to drink lau-lao from clay jugs using long straws. *Beer Lao* is a light lager with 5 percent alcohol content. It is consumed ice cold.

Lao coffee is excellent. Most of it comes from the fertile Bolaven Plateau in southern Laos. Roasted and ground, it is filtered with hot water in a socklike bag before being served in cafés and restaurants. The Lao prefer their coffee thick and sweet, so sugar and condensed milk are freely added. You can also enjoy it cold by adding crushed ice. Traditionally coffee is served with a complimentary glass of *naam sa* (nam SAH), or weak Chinese tea. Both black Indian tea and cured or green Chinese tea are common in Laos.

Bottles of traditional homemade herbal liquor contain the bodies of pickled snakes, scorpions, and other poisonous animals.

INTERNET LINKS

https://www.asian-recipe.com/laos
This site provides background on the country as well as recipes.

http://factsanddetails.com/southeast-asia/Laos/sub5_3b/ entry-2957.html
http://factsanddetails.com/southeast-asia/Laos/sub5_3b/ entry-2958.html
These pages provide an in-depth look at Lao cuisine and food culture.

http://www.npr.org/2011/10/18/141465353/colonizers-influence-infuses-southeast-asian-cuisine
This article discusses the connection between history and food.

LARB GAI (CHICKEN LARB)

4 tablespoons raw Thai glutinous rice

⅔ cup (160 milliliters) fresh lime juice

¼ cup (60 mL) fish sauce (nam pla)

1 Tbsp sugar

2 teaspoons Thai roasted chili paste in oil or chili-garlic sauce

1 Tbsp vegetable oil

1 ¼ pounds (563 g) ground chicken

½ cup (15 g) thinly sliced green onions

3 thinly sliced shallots

3 Tbsp minced fresh lemongrass

1 Tbsp minced Thai chilies or serrano chilies

⅓ cup (10 g) chopped fresh cilantro leaves

⅓ cup (10 g) chopped fresh mint leaves

2 small heads Boston lettuce, separated into leaves

Cook the 4 tablespoons of rice in a dry, small, heavy skillet over moderately high heat, stirring constantly, until golden brown, 4 to 6 minutes (rice will smoke). Grind to a coarse powder in an electric coffee/spice grinder or with a mortar and pestle.

Whisk next 4 ingredients in medium bowl to blend; set aside.

Heat oil in heavy large skillet over medium heat. Add chicken. Stir fry until cooked through, breaking up meat with spoon, about 2 minutes. Stir in ground rice, green onions and next 3 ingredients, cook about 1 minute. Remove from heat. Stir in sauce, cilantro and mint. Season with salt and pepper.

Spoon into lettuce leaves; serve. Accompany with tomato and cucumber, coarsely chopped, and Thai glutinous rice, cooked according to package directions.

KHAO NIAO MAMUANG (COCONUT STICKY RICE WITH MANGO)

1 cup (200 grams) Thai sweet sticky rice

1 (14-ounce; 400ml) can full-fat coconut milk, blended well.

½ cup (3 ½ ounces; 100g) sugar

Kosher salt

2 teaspoons cornstarch

2 mangoes (Ataúlfo mangoes, if possible), peeled, pitted, and sliced

Toasted sesame seeds, for garnish

In a large bowl, cover rice with water by several inches and let stand at room temperature 1 hour or up to overnight.

Drain and rinse the rice. Line a steamer with moistened cheesecloth or a clean kitchen towel. Add the rice. Bring the water to a boil over medium flame, cover tightly, and steam the rice for 25 to 30 minutes.

Meanwhile, in a small saucepan, bring the coconut milk to a simmer over medium heat, stirring frequently. Whisk in the sugar and a large pinch of salt until dissolved. The coconut milk should taste salty-sweet.

Transfer cooked rice to a large bowl and pour half of coconut milk mixture on top (it will look like too much liquid). Stir and cover with plastic wrap, and let stand until liquid is absorbed, about 30 minutes. (You can let it stand up to 2 hours at room temperature.)

To serve, mound coconut rice onto plates and arrange sliced mango alongside. Drizzle remaining coconut cream over the rice and garnish with toasted sesame seeds. Serve right away.

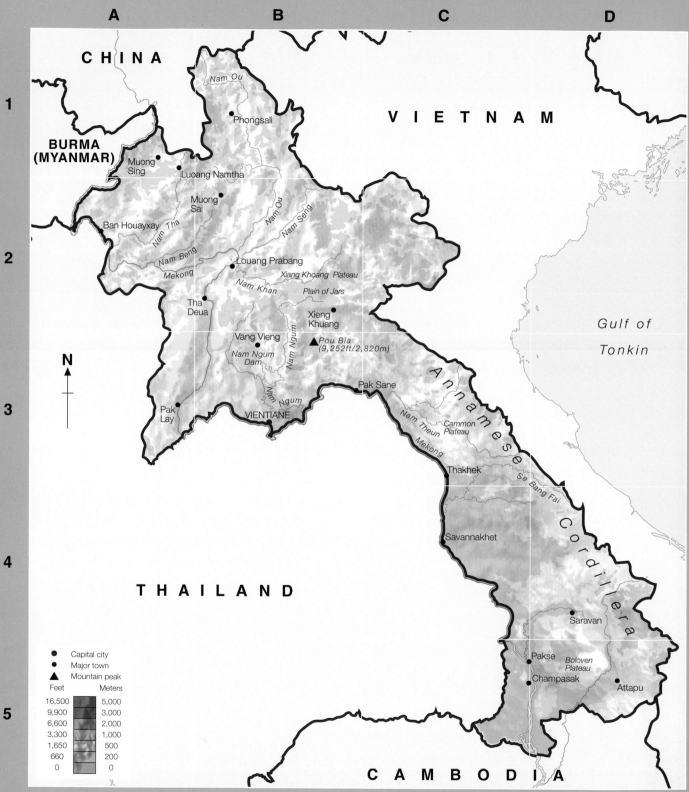

A   B   C   D

CHINA

1   Nam Ou
                    Phongsali

BURMA
(MYANMAR)
           Muong
           Sing
              Luoang Namtha

                 Muong
                 Sai   Nam Seng

           Ban Houayxay

                                    Nam Ou
2   VIETNAM
                Nam Beng

          Mekong   Louang Prabang
                                    Xiang Khoang Plateau
                         Nam Khan   Plain of Jars
              Tha
              Deua   Xieng
                                      Khuang
                                   ▲ Pou Bia
                    Vang Vieng   (9,252ft/2,820m)
              N   Nam Ngum Dam
                                         Pak Sane
3   Nam Ngum
              Pak   Gulf of
              Lay   VIENTIANE   Nam Theun   Tonkin
                                         Cammon
                                         Plateau

                                        Thakhek   Se Bang Fai

                                         Mekong

4   Savannakhet
        THAILAND

                                              Saravan

                                         Pakse   Boloven
5   ● Capital city   Plateau
    ● Major town   Champasak
    ▲ Mountain peak   Attapu
    Feet   Meters
    16,500   5,000
    9,900   3,000
    6,600   2,000
    3,300   1,000
    1,650   500
    660   200
    0   0   CAMBODIA

Annamese Cordillera, C3, D4
Attapu, D5

Ban Houayxay, A2
Bolaven Plateau, D5
Burma (Myanmar), A1—A2

Cambodia, B5, C5, D5
Cammon Plateau, C3
Champasak, D5
China, A1, B1

Gulf of Tonkin, C2—C3, D1—D4

Louang Prabang, B2
Louang Namtha, A1

Mekong, A2, B2, C3
Muong Sai, B2
Muong Sing, A1

Nam Beng, A2
Nam Khan, B2
Nam Ngum, B3
Nam Ngum Dam, B3
Nam Ou, B1—B2
Nam Seng, B2
Nam Tha, A2
Nam Theun, C3

Pak Lay, A3
Pak Sane, B3
Pakse, D5
Phongsali, B1
Plain of Jars, B2
Pou Bia, B3

Saravan, D4

Savannakhet, C4
Se Bang Fai, C3, D4

Thailand, A2—A5, B3—B5, C3—C5
Tha Deua, B2
Thakhek, C3

Vang Vieng, B3
Vientiane, B3
Vietnam, B1—B2, C1—C3, D1—D5

Xieng Khuang, B2
Xieng Khuang Plateau, B2

ECONOMIC LAOS

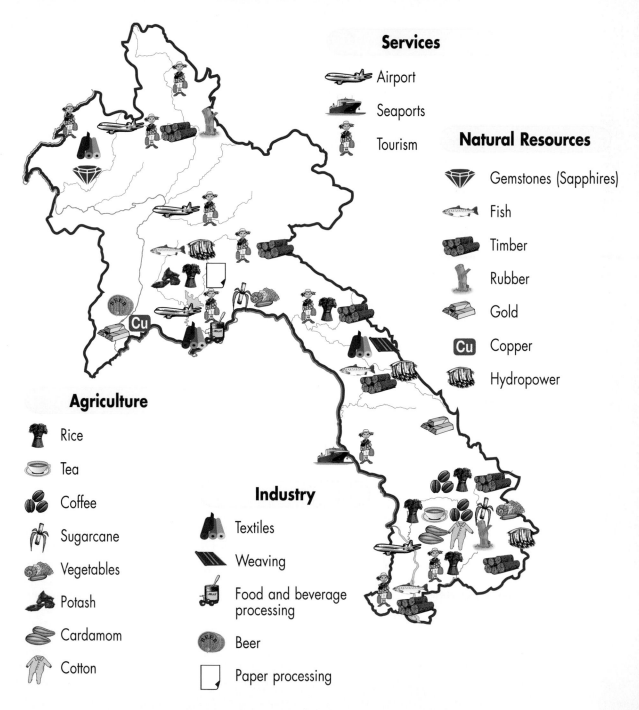

Services

✈ Airport

🚢 Seaports

🧳 Tourism

Natural Resources

💎 Gemstones (Sapphires)

🐟 Fish

🪵 Timber

🪵 Rubber

🪙 Gold

Cu Copper

⚡ Hydropower

Agriculture

🌾 Rice

☕ Tea

☕ Coffee

🌱 Sugarcane

🥗 Vegetables

⛏ Potash

🫘 Cardamom

👕 Cotton

Industry

🧵 Textiles

🪡 Weaving

🥫 Food and beverage processing

🍺 Beer

📄 Paper processing

ABOUT THE ECONOMY

TYPE OF ECONOMY
communist

GROSS DOMESTIC PRODUCT (GDP)
(official exchange rate)
$13.79 billion (2016)

GDP GROWTH
6.9 percent (2016)

INFLATION RATE
2 percent (2016)

CURRENCY
Kip (LAK)
US$1 = 8,306 LAK (September 2017)
The kip is available only in paper notes.
Laos has no coins.

NATURAL RESOURCES
timber, hydropower, gypsum, tin, gold, gemstones

AGRICULTURAL PRODUCTS
sweet potatoes, vegetables, corn, coffee, sugarcane, tobacco, cotton, tea, peanuts, rice; cassava (manioc, tapioca), water buffalo, pigs, cattle, poultry

INDUSTRY
mining (copper, tin, gold, gypsum); timber, electric power, agricultural processing, rubber, construction, garments, cement, tourism

MAJOR EXPORTS
wood products, coffee, electricity, tin, copper, gold, cassava

MAJOR IMPORTS
machinery and equipment, vehicles, fuel, consumer goods

MAIN TRADE PARTNERS
Thailand, China, Vietnam

WORKFORCE
3.5 million (2016)
73.1 percent in agriculture
6.1 percent in industry
20.6 percent in services (2012)

UNEMPLOYMENT RATE
1.3 percent (2013)

POPULATION BELOW POVERTY LINE
22 percent (2013)

CULTURAL LAOS

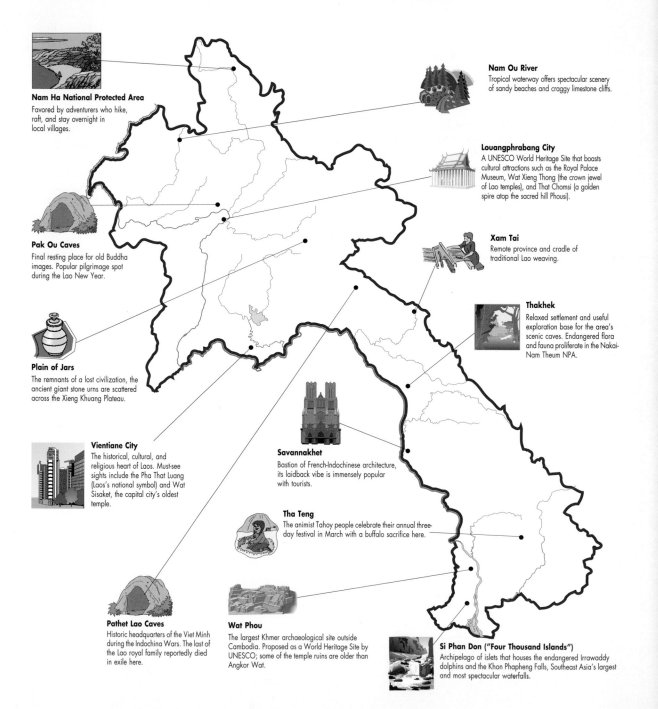

Nam Ha National Protected Area
Favored by adventurers who hike, raft, and stay overnight in local villages.

Pak Ou Caves
Final resting place for old Buddha images. Popular pilgrimage spot during the Lao New Year.

Plain of Jars
The remnants of a lost civilization, the ancient giant stone urns are scattered across the Xieng Khuang Plateau.

Nam Ou River
Tropical waterway offers spectacular scenery of sandy beaches and craggy limestone cliffs.

Louangphrabang City
A UNESCO World Heritage Site that boasts cultural attractions such as the Royal Palace Museum, Wat Xieng Thong (the crown jewel of Lao temples), and That Chomsi (a golden spire atop the sacred hill Phousi).

Xam Tai
Remote province and cradle of traditional Lao weaving.

Thakhek
Relaxed settlement and useful exploration base for the area's scenic caves. Endangered flora and fauna proliferate in the Nakai-Nam Theum NPA.

Vientiane City
The historical, cultural, and religious heart of Laos. Must-see sights include the Pha That Luang (Laos's national symbol) and Wat Sisaket, the capital city's oldest temple.

Savannakhet
Bastion of French-Indochinese architecture, its laidback vibe is immensely popular with tourists.

Tha Teng
The animist Tahoy people celebrate their annual three-day festival in March with a buffalo sacrifice here.

Pathet Lao Caves
Historic headquarters of the Viet Minh during the Indochina Wars. The last of the Lao royal family reportedly died in exile here.

Wat Phou
The largest Khmer archaeological site outside Cambodia. Proposed as a World Heritage Site by UNESCO; some of the temple ruins are older than Angkor Wat.

Si Phan Don ("Four Thousand Islands")
Archipelago of islets that houses the endangered Irrawaddy dolphins and the Khon Phapheng Falls, Southeast Asia's largest and most spectacular waterfalls.

ABOUT THE CULTURE

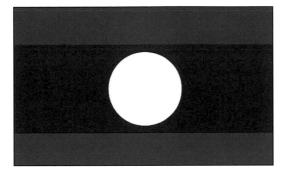

OFFICIAL NAME
Lao People's Democratic Republic (LPDR)

FLAG DESCRIPTION
Three horizontal bands—red stripes at the top and the bottom, with a central blue band that is twice as wide. A white circle sits in the center of the blue band. The red symbolizes blood shed during the country's long civil war, and the blue represents the Mekong River. The white circle symbolizes the people's unity.

INDEPENDENCE
July 19, 1949

CAPITAL
Vientiane (Vieng Chan)

MAJOR CITIES
Vientiane, Luang Prabang, Pakse, Savannakhet

POPULATION
7.1 million (2017)

BIRTHRATE
23.6 births per 1,000 Lao (2017)

INFANT MORTALITY RATE
51.4 deaths/1,000 live births

LIFE EXPECTANCY
64.3 years (2016)

ETHNIC GROUPS
Lao 53.2 percent, Khmou 11 percent, Hmong 9.2 percent, Phouthay 3.4 percent, Tai 3.1 percent, Makong 2.5 percent, Katong 2.2 percent, Lue 2 percent, Akha 1.8 percent, other 11.6 percent
Note: the Laos Government officially recognizes forty-nine ethnic groups, but the total number of ethnic groups is estimated to be well over two hundred (2015)

RELIGIONS
Buddhist 64.7 percent, Christian 1.7 percent, none 31.4 percent, other/not stated 2.1 percent (2015)

MAIN LANGUAGES
Lao (official), French, English, various ethnic languages

LITERACY RATE
79.9 percent (2015)

TIMELINE

IN LAOS	IN THE WORLD
10,000 BCE Descended from hunter-gatherers, the early people of Laos settle along the Mekong River.	**323 BCE** Alexander the Great's empire stretches from Greece to India.
CE 100 Indian settlers establish foundation of Theravada Buddhism.	
900 The Khmer come into power and establish Angkor as their capital.	**1206–1368** Genghis Khan unifies the Mongols and starts conquest of the world. At its height, the Mongol Empire under Kublai Khan stretches from China to Persia and parts of Europe and Russia.
1353 FaNgum conquers Luang Prabang and establishes Lan Xang.	
1479 Vietnam invades Lan Xang.	**1558–1603** Reign of Elizabeth I of England
1563 King Setthathirat moves the capital of Lan Xang from Luang Prabang to Vieng Chan (Vientiane).	
1571 Setthathirat dies. Burma invades and occupies Lan Xang.	
1637–1694 Lan Xang's golden age: King SoulignaVongsare establishes kingdom as an independent state.	
1700s–1800s Period of instability.Lan Xang separates into three kingdoms, which are repeatedly invaded.	**1776** US Declaration of Independence
1826 Lao king Chao Anou is killed after a failed rebellion against Siam. Vientiane is razed.	**1789–1799** The French Revolution
1893 France colonizes Laos.	**1914** World War I begins.
1939 Japanese forces control Laos.	**1939** World War II begins.
1945–1946 World War II ends. Start of First Indochina War.	**1945** The United States drops atomic bombs on Hiroshima and Nagasaki.

IN LAOS		IN THE WORLD
1949–1950 Laos gains independence from France.		**1949** The North Atlantic Treaty Organization (NATO) is formed.
1954 Vietnam defeats France, leading to Communist takeover in Indochina.		**1955–1975** Vietnam War (Second Indochina War)
1975 Lao People's Democratic Republic (LPDR), a Communist state, is established.		**1969** Neil Armstrong becomes the first human to walk on the moon.
1986 Introduction of a market economy.		**1986** Nuclear power disaster at Chernobyl in Ukraine
1992 Laos establishes relations with United States.		**1991** Breakup of the Soviet Union
1994 Friendship Bridge links Laos with Thailand.		
1997 Laos joins the Association of Southeast Asian Nations (ASEAN).		**2001** Terrorists crash planes in New York, Washington, DC, and Pennsylvania.
		2003 War in Iraq begins.
2008 Save the Children reports 69 percent of Lao children lack basic health care.		**2008** US elects first African American president, Barack Obama.
2013 Laos becomes member of World Trade Organization.		
		2015–2016 ISIS launches terror attacks in Belgium and France.
2016 Bounnhang Vorachit becomes president, succeeding Choummaly Sayasone.		
2016 President Barack Obama, first sitting US president to visit Laos, commits $90 million to help clear unexploded bombs.		
2017 Kenya-based group Save the Elephants reports Laos is now the world's fastest growing market for illegal ivory.		**2017** Donald Trump becomes US president. Britain begins Brexit process of leaving the EU.

GLOSSARY

baci (BAH-see, sukhwan)
Ritual held to celebrate special occasions such as marriages, births, and homecomings.

boun (boon)
Festival.

jataka (jah-TAK-er)
Incarnations of the Buddha.

kampi (kem-PI)
Lao manuscripts, usually engraved on palm leaves and threaded together with cord.

kha dong (kaa DONG)
Dowry or bride price paid by the groom.

khene (ken)
Hand organ or harmonica made from varying lengths of bamboo tubes.

khongvong (ker-ONG VON)
Horseshoe-shaped musical instrument made up of sixteen small bronze gongs that are struck with wooden mallets.

khuy (KOO)
A type of bamboo flute.

kwan (KWA-ang)
Spirits that protect the body.

laap (laap) or larb
A traditional ceremonial dish, served on special occasions or to honored guests. It is made from finely minced beef and venison, with chopped mint and lemon juice.

lau-lao (LA-oo-lao)
Fermented rice wine.

mudra
Attitude, or the way the Buddha images are represented.

naga (NAR-ger)
Mythical water serpent that resembles a cobra. In Lao it is refered to as nak.

nangnat (ner-ANG nat)
Small xylophone.

phi (PEE)
Guardian spirit.

takraw (TAHK-raw)
Traditional game played with a hollow cane ball.

wat (what) or vat
Pagoda or temple.

FOR FURTHER INFORMATION

BOOKS

Fadiman, Anne. *The Spirit Catches You and You Fall Down: A Hmong Child, Her American Doctors, and the Collision of Two Cultures.* New York: Farrar, Straus, and Giroux, 1998.

Hamilton-Merritt, Jane. *Tragic Mountains: The Hmong, the Americans, and the Secret Wars for Laos, 1942—1992.* Bloomington: Indiana University Press, 1993.

Kurlantzick, Joshua. *A Great Place to Have a War: America in Laos and the Birth of a Military CIA.* New York: Simon & Schuster, 2017.

Syhabout, James and John Birdsall. *Hawker Fare: Stories & Recipes from a Refugee Chef's Thai Isan & Lao Roots.* New York: Anthony Bourdain/Ecco, 2018.

Warner, Roger. *Shooting at the Moon: The Story of America's Clandestine War in Laos.* Hanover, Germany: Steerforth Press, 2006

Yang, Kao Kalia. *The Latehomecomer: A Hmong Family Memoir.* Minneapolis, Minn.: Coffee House Press, 2008.

ONLINE

BBC News, Laos country profile. http://www.bbc.com/news/world-asia-pacific-15351898

BBC Travel. Laos. http://www.bbc.com/travel/asia/laos

CIA World Factbook, Laos. https://www.cia.gov/library/publications/the-world-factbook/geos/la.html

Facts and Details. Laos. http://factsanddetails.com/southeast-asia

Lonely Planet, Laos. https://www.lonelyplanet.com/laos

Radio Free Asia. Laos section. http://www.rfa.org/english/news/laos

FILMS

The Betrayal. Cinema Guild, 2009.

The Rocket. Kino Lorber Films, 2013.

MUSIC

Bamboo Voices: folk music from Laos. Khamvong Insixienmai Ensemble, Latitudes/Music of the World, 1996.

Laos: Traditional Music of the South, UNESCO, 1973; Smithsonian Folkways, 2014

BIBLIOGRAPHY

Allman, T. D., "Laos Finds New Life After the Bombs." *National Geographic*, August 2015. http://ngm.nationalgeographic.com/2015/08/laos/allman-text

Ballentine, Sandra. "In Laos, It's All About Weave." *The New York Times*, September 23, 2007. http://www.nytimes.com/2007/09/23/travel/tmagazine/10get-sourcing-txt.html?mcubz=0

BBC News. Laos profile - timeline. http://www.bbc.com/news/world-asia-pacific-15355605

CIA World Factbook. Laos. https://www.cia.gov/library/publications/the-world-factbook/geos/la.html

Facts and Details. Laos. http://factsanddetails.com/southeast-asia

Freedom House. Freedom of the Press 2015, Laos. https://freedomhouse.org/report/freedom-press/2015/laos

Gladstone, Rick. "Casualties From Cluster Bombs More Than Doubled Last Year, Treaty Monitor Says." *The New York Times*, August 31, 2017. https://www.nytimes.com/2017/08/31/world/middleeast/casualties-cluster-bombs-syria-yemen-laos.html

Hance, Jeremy. "Corruption still plundering forests in Laos for furniture." Mongabay, September 26, 2012. https://news.mongabay.com/2012/09/corruption-still-plundering-forests-in-laos-for-furniture

Kolinovsky, Sarah. "The Bombing of Laos: By the Numbers." ABC News, September 6, 2016. http://abcnews.go.com/International/bombing-laos-numbers/story?id=41890565

Phomnuny, Petsamone. "Laos Expects to Have 100 Hydropower Plants by 2020." Mekong Eye, July 12, 2017. https://www.mekongeye.com/2017/07/12/laos-expects-to-have-100-hydropower-plants-by-2020

Radio Free Asia. "New Lao Prime Minister Issues Ban on Timber Exports." May 17, 2016. http://www.rfa.org/english/news/laos/new-lao-prime-minister-issues-ban-on-timber-exports-05172016152448.html

Turow, Eve. "Colonizers' Influence Infuses Southeast Asian Cuisine." NPR, October 19, 2011. http://www.npr.org/2011/10/18/141465353/colonizers-influence-infuses-southeast-asian-cuisine

Xinhuanet.com, Asia & Pacific Edition. "Laos to reforest over 37,000 hectares of land in 2017." January 11, 2017. http://news.xinhuanet.com/english/2017-01/11/c_135974552.htm

INDEX

INDEX